CURRICULUM
BUILDING
FOR ADULT
LEARNING BY JOHN R. VERDUIN, JR.

SOUTHERN ILLINOIS UNIVERSITY PRESS   Carbondale and Edwardsville

Feffer & Simons, Inc.: London and Amsterdam

Library of Congress Cataloging in Publication Data

Verduin, John R
  Curriculum building for adult learning.

  Bibliography: p.
  Includes index.
  1. Adult education--Curricula--Planning. I. Title.
LC5219.V47   374'.01   79-23111
ISBN 0-8093-0960-2

Contents

Preface

This book is built on the assumption that all people
involved in the adult learning process are curriculum
workers to some extent. Regardless of our position as
teachers, administrators, or special personnel in adult
basic and adult continuing education, business and
industrial learning programs, prison, hospital, or other
social service area learning programs, programs for the
elderly, or any adult learning area, we deal with curriculum or program issues, concerns, and problems and
make improvements or changes from time to time. Some
of us are involved in rather large, formal improvement
and/or developmental efforts and some are making day-
to-day or smaller improvements. Whatever the case, many
of our educational efforts deal with curriculum or
program development ideas. Since much of our professional time is and should be devoted to thinking about
and fostering curriculum development and improvement,
it seems that perhaps some theoretical construct about
a curriculum would be important and helpful to guide us
in our activities.

Associated with this idea is another assumption
that we do not have total awareness about or understand
fully what a curriculum is, what are its elements and

parts, and what factors should be considered when
working with a curriculum. Without such knowledge we
may be spinning our wheels in curriculum and program
development activities and developing poorly coordinated, loosely structured, and incomplete experiences
for our adult clients. With a better knowledge based
on what the nature of the curriculum is, we can hope-
fully make better decisions and can provide more complete experiences which can be coordinated and checked
closely for their value. In the absence of a systematic
structure, curriculum work can be spotty at best and
result in a scissors-and-pastepot type of activity.
Consideration should be given to all aspects of the
curriculum as development proceeds so that all parts
are in consonance and a more complete system is developed.

This book is addressed to adult curriculum workers
in their educational settings. And by this I mean the
professional staff, the adult teachers, administrators,
and special personnel of a program, school, or center.
Since they are the ones that carry out and lead curriculum experiences, they should be aware of the structure of the curriculum and should be involved in improvement activities.

Considerable curriculum rethinking and developmental
activities are taking place at this time in the dynamic
field of adult learning. Some of this has come from
the competency-based movement and some has come from
simply meeting the emerging needs of adults in such
areas as adult basic education, vocational training
and retraining, and enrichment and leisure activities.
This will continue as long as there are adult clients
with their diverse needs to serve, and continuous

curriculum work will be required. And continuous review, development, and evaluation are not only healthy
but imperative to insure that our curriculum and program offerings are meeting the needs of adult students
in a dynamic, highly technical, democratic society. A
guide to curriculum structure and organization will
help in this continuous process and will make curriculum
workers aware of the various considerations and elements
found in a curriculum.

This book presents only a guide, a structure, a
skeleton. Adult curriculum workers in their professional
situations have the task of putting the meat on the
bones. Decisions about the nature of the curriculum
should come from the adult curriculum workers and others
involved in the process. This volume will help in the
decision-making process by identifying the important
variables that mediate in the curriculum-building
process, but it will not tell how to treat those
variables. For example, it will suggest and discuss at
length the importance of goals for adult learning, but
will not suggest what goals should be there. This is
the task of the adult education curriculum workers.

The general curriculum model advanced and explained
in this text was introduced in another book of mine
(Verduin, Harry Miller, and Charles Greer, Adults
Teaching Adults: Principles and Strategies [Austin,
Tex.: Learning Concepts, 1977], ch. 3). In this present
text greater explication is afforded for use by practicing adult educators.

With the definition and explication of the five
major elements in a curriculum, parts of this book may
be used in isolation if necessary. In other words, the

section on goals may be utilized if curriculum workers are desirous of reviewing the stated goals for a given program. Or, certain audiences may wish to use the instruction and content or organization section in improving this phase of their program. The models in those sections will lend precision during an improvement or review process.

Chapter 1 introduces the general curriculum model and its various elements. The following five chapters describe and explain the five major elements in the model. The concluding chapter of the book offers some ideas on the application of the general model and various elements for use by the practicing adult education curriculum worker.

John R. Verduin, Jr.
Carbondale, Illinois
September 15, 1979

Acknowledgments

I should like to thank Arthur E. Lean, Professor Emeritus, Southern Illinois University at Carbondale, for an early review of the manuscript of this book and encouragement in its development and publication. The inspiring example of the lifelong work of Asahel D. Woodruff has been deeply appreciated, as has been the gracious permission of Elizabeth J. Simpson and the publisher, Gryphon House, to quote from her Psychomotor Taxonomy and Instrumentation materials as outlined in her essay "The Classification of Educational Objectives in the Psychomotor Domain," in The Psychomotor Domain, Floyd Urbach, ed. (Washington, D.C.: Gryphon House, 1972), pp. 43-56. I should also like to thank Mary Jane Schaaf, Ann Teel, and Betty McNeely for their continuous effort in typing and retyping the manuscript. And the encouragement of my two adult education colleagues, Harry G. Miller and Charles E. Greer, will always be appreciated. Thanks to all of you.

Grateful acknowledgment is extended for permission to quote from the following sources: John R. Verduin, Jr., Conceptual Models in Teacher Education: An Approach to Teaching and Learning, copyright © 1967 by The American Association of Colleges for Teacher Education;

from Preparing Objectives for Programmed Instruction, by Robert F. Mager, copyright © 1961 by Fearon-Pitman Publishers, Inc., 6 Davis Drive, Belmont, CA 94002, reprinted by permission; David R. Krathwohl, "Stating Objectives Appropriately for Program, for Curriculum, and for Instructional Materials Development," Journal of Teacher Education 16, no. 1 (March 1965): 83-92, copyright, 1965, The American Association of Colleges for Teacher Education; from Taxonomy of Educational Objectives. The Classification of Educational Goals, Handbook 1: Cognitive Domain, by Benjamin S. Bloom, et al., copyright © 1956 by Longman Inc., reprinted with permission of Longman; from Taxonomy of Educational Objectives. The Classification of Educational Goals, Handbook 2: Affective Domain, by David R. Krathwohl et al., copyright © 1964 by Longman Inc., reprinted with permission of Longman; Newton S. Metfessel, William B. Michael, and Donald A. Kirsner, "Instrumentation of Bloom's and Krathwohl's Taxonomies for the Writing of Educational Objectives," Psychology in the Schools 6, no. 3 (July 1969): 227-31, copyright 1969, Clinical Psychology Publishing Company, Inc.; John P. De Cecco, William R. Crawford, The Psychology of Learning and Instruction: Educational Psychology, 2nd ed., © 1974, reprinted by permission of Prentice-Hall, Inc., Englewood Cliffs, New Jersey; Asahel D. Woodruff, "Putting Subject Matter into Conceptual Form" (Paper prepared for TEAM Project meeting [which Project was sponsored by The American Association of Colleges for Teacher Education, which Association grants permission to reprint in this volume], Washington, D.C., Feb. 6, 1964); and from Handbook on Formative and Summative

Evaluation of Student Learning, by Benjamin S. Bloom, J. Thomas Hastings, and George F. Madaus, copyright © 1971 by McGraw-Hill, Inc., used with permission of McGraw-Hill Book Company.

Finally, I must express my deep appreciation to my family--Janet, John, and Susan--for their continuous encouragement and support in this writing effort.

CURRICULUM BUILDING
FOR ADULT LEARNING

1 / Introduction

A Models Approach. Working in the area of curriculum, through designing, development and/or improvement activities, is much like the process of teaching or administering; it involves numerous decisions to be made by the professional adult educator and colleagues. Just as the adult teacher makes a series of decisions on questions to be asked in class, materials to be used, strategies for achieving specific objectives, evaluation techniques, and so forth, adult education curriculum workers must make decisions in a variety of areas as they attempt to build the best possible learning experience package for the adult clients in their charge. Adult curriculum workers must decide not only on what experiences, but why the experiences, how to program them in, and how to assess the effect of the experiences on adult students' total behaviors. For example, curriculum people should interpret various sociocultural phenomena and make decisions regarding their effect on adults and the adult education curriculum. They must express certain value judgments and make decisions on what is important or of value for their adult clients, the school, and society. They must design and organize learning experiences, and finally must decide on some means of measurement to assess the value of the experiences on adult students. The adult curriculum worker and professional colleagues are, therefore, confronted with many decisions on the what, why, how, and when in curriculum development activities.

The decision-making process can be made considerably easier if some systematic structure is present which identifies the mediating variables in a given situation and places them in a consistent and coherent relationship. This systematic structure or model can provide awareness of the important variables in a situation and thus can afford the professional educator the opportunity for analysis of information, the synthesis of ideas, and finally the judgment or evaluation of what is worthwhile for the curriculum. This is the decision-making process.

A model, although it reflects the values of its developer, should in essence be value free and should provide the means for analysis of a given situation while not really providing any "set answers" to the situation. In this case an adult education curriculum worker should view the professional situation (the curriculum) through a theoretical or conceptual model and then make the decision as to what should or should not appear in a certain curriculum for a certain group of adult students. The value of using models for decision making in curriculum work is that it brings to the level of awareness the important, mediating variables in a given situation. Once the variables are identified and examined, then decisions about them can be made. Further, a model or set of models can have broad application to various levels of education. For example, a model for stating appropriate goals or objectives will have application for any kind of instruction, be it technical, adult basic education, or special education for adults. In this case the broad application will aid adult education curriculum workers at any level in the identification of the variables as they foster decisions on goals, even though the model does not suggest what the goals should be.

Finally, a model or set of models should provide for the internal consistency necessary in appropriate professional situations like the curriculum. In doing this a model identifies the variables and places them in an appropriate relationship to one another. This should bring more order and consistency to the total experiences to which adults are exposed and, again, is of value to curriculum workers.

Working with the curriculum, or all of the learning experiences that come under the direction of a given adult center, program, or school, is a massive job. With the assistance of some theoretical frameworks or models, more effective decisions can be made which will make the task easier and result in better learning experiences for the adult clients. This is a most important task for adult curriculum workers, be they teachers, administrators, and/or people outside the profession, and it is to this point that the following effort is devoted.

A Model for Curriculum Structure. An overall view of the general curriculum model[1] at the outset is essential for adult curriculum workers in order that they may view the various elements, sub-elements, and their relationship in their entirety. This section will present

an overview of the structure of a curriculum with sub-
sequent chapters focusing in detail on the major elements defined.

The basic curriculum model is an extension and modification of the ideas advanced earlier by Tyler[2] and
Taba.[3] Tyler suggested several questions that required
answering as one thinks about and works in curriculum
activities. Taba presented similar ideas about curriculum organization with emphasis on consideration for
developmental efforts. In taking these ideas and ex-
panding on them, a curriculum might be viewed generally
as a five-element structure.

Goals. Initially the curriculum should contain a statement of goals about what is important for students to
learn. This element should answer the question, "What
is worth learning in the adult view?" The goals are an
expression of what is deemed important for adults to
focus on and thus give direction for the entire learning experience. They set the stage for what follows as
everything else should be contingent on goal statements. As will be noted later, educational goals or
objectives (used interchangeably in this volume) can
be expressed at three different levels corresponding
to the different levels of curriculum development and
should be considered in three different domains; cognitive, affective, and psychomotor.

A representation of the first element appears
thus:

Goals (What is worth learning in the adult view?)

General level	Cognitive domain
Intermediate level	Affective domain
Specific level	Psychomotor domain

FIGURE 1.1 *Goals*

Instruction and Content Organization. Following goals, the second major element of a curriculum is the instructional activities and the organizational means of accomplishing the goals. This major element can answer the question, "How will the goals be accomplished?" and focuses on such areas as instructional processes, the content to be taught, the materials to be used, and various other concerns of the instructional process. This element can actually be viewed as the delivery system designed to fulfill the goals.

This element may be viewed schematically as such:

Instructional Activities and Organization (How will the goals be accomplished?)

Instruction
Content Organization

FIGURE 1.2 *Instruction and Content Organization*

Evaluation. A third major component of the curriculum model is that of evaluation which answers the general question, "Were the goals accomplished at the three levels?" This assessment process attempts to gather information to see if the adult learners involved have achieved the goals as a result of the instructional process, and it includes internal and external data collection of a formative and summative nature geared to the previously suggested goals. In this case evaluation is concerned primarily with adult student growth or achievement in the various domains.

The representation of this element appears thus:

Evaluation (Were the goals accomplished at three levels?)

General level goals					
	⎧	Internal means	⎧	Formative data	
Intermediate level goals	⎨		⎨		
		External means		Summative data	
Specific level goals	⎩		⎩		

FIGURE 1.3 *Evaluation*

The first three elements of the curriculum combined and placed in proper order actually form what might be defined as the design of the curriculum. The elements when analyzed and filled in lead to a definite curriculum design of one sort or another. They should provide a complete and coherent set of learning experiences for adult students which can go in one rather specific direction or in a variety of different directions. However, they should represent a definite and clearly thought-through design for a group of adult learners to accomplish something in an educational setting.

With the definition of the first three elements of the curriculum a graphic representation of a partial model (curriculum design) is shown on page 7.

In viewing the curriculum "design" it will be noted that the goals actually set the stage and provide the direction. The instructional activities and

organization are so designed to help accomplish the
purposes (goals) of the curriculum, and the evaluation
procedures gather information to see if the goals were
accomplished. The arrows between the major elements
indicate the direction or flow in a curriculum design.
They also show the internal consistency, order, and
interdependence of these major elements of the curriculum design.

Goals (What is worth learning in the adult view?)

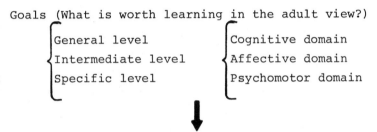

General level   Cognitive domain
Intermediate level   Affective domain
Specific level   Psychomotor domain

Instructional Activities and Organization (How will
the goals be accomplished?)

Instruction
Content Organization

Evaluation (Were the goals accomplished at three levels?)

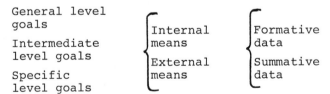

General level
goals
                Internal   Formative
Intermediate   means   data
level goals
                External   Summative
Specific   means   data
level goals

FIGURE 1.4 *Curriculum Design*

Rationale. These major elements would be all that is
necessary in the curriculum of an adult educational

program or institution if it were to function and operate in a social-cultural-philosophical vacuum. However, in American society different values, perceptions,
interpretations, beliefs, and persuasions are present
and come into play when one thinks about an adult institution and what should be its purpose and mission.
A free society provides the opportunity through various forms of representation to suggest directions for
an institution such as the school. For the adult school
there is generally a reason for the curriculum going
in one educational direction or for going in a variety
of directions--or at least, there should be. The reasons precede any statement of goals because they in
essence describe why the ultimate direction and pattern
(curriculum design) were taken. Reasons are actually a
justification and an explanation (a position paper, if
you will) for a given direction, pattern, or design.
In the curriculum the reasons are called a rationale.

The rationale sets forth an exposition of the fundamental bases for a selected curriculum design. It
should describe how a given set of individuals, professional and lay, believe and feel about people, the
objects and events in society, and the meanings that
they have for a curriculum for adult students. The beliefs and feelings are derived from a careful analysis
of psychological-philosophical considerations and
sociological-anthropological considerations. The former
is suggested because of the many values related to
adult students, purposes of education, social milieu,
and so forth. The latter is suggested because of the
sociocultural forces that play upon adult learners,
other people, schools, and curricula.

Careful analyses of these factors are imperative for adult education curriculum workers as they begin to specify a rationale or reason for all curriculum experiences. Upon the consideration of these many factors, as explicated later, the curriculum may take the shape of a vocationally oriented curriculum or a society-oriented curriculum or a "competency-based" curriculum or what have you, because there is a reason based on a careful analysis for going to a certain set of learning experiences (curriculum design). This consideration of a rationale also lifts adult education curriculum workers from that of technicians to true professional status because they must provide the "whys" for such professional curriculum development activity.

A brief representation of the rationale dimension is as follows:

Rationale (What do we believe and feel about people, students, schooling, society, and other environmental phenomena and their meaning for an adult school program?)

Psycho-Philosophical Factors

Sociocultural Factors

FIGURE 1.5 *Rationale*

Adding the rationale dimension to the basic curriculum design model would cause the partial curriculum model to appear as shown on page 10.

Rationale (What do we believe and feel about people, students, schooling, society, and other environmental phenomena and their meaning for an adult school program?)

Psycho-Philosophical Factors

Sociocultural Factors

Goals (What is worth learning in the adult view?)

General level   ⌠Cognitive domain

Intermediate level ⟨Affective domain

Specific level   ⌡Psychomotor domain

Instructional Activities and Organization (How will the goals be accomplished?)

Instruction

Content Organization

Evaluation (Were the goals accomplished at three levels?)

General level
goals   ⌠Internal   ⌠Formative
                      means   data
Intermediate
level goals   ⟨   ⟨
                      External   Summative
Specific   means   data
level goals   ⌡   ⌡

FIGURE 1.6 *Partial Curriculum Model*

A reversible arrow between the rationale and the goals is suggested because of the reciprocal influence between the reasons and the actual curriculum design.

The reasons (rationale) are reflected in the goals of the curriculum and the goals are also reflected in the reasons for such a curriculum endeavor. The two major elements must operate in consonance with one another and must indicate a clear compatibility if the entire curriculum is to be effective. The reversible arrow might further imply that a constant reexamination of these two major and important elements is not only necessary for compatibility and consistency, but to see if they are doing what adult education curriculum workers and others feel that they should be doing. After all, these two elements provide the direction and reasoning for all classroom and other learning activities.

Outside Political Forces. The above model would suffice for adult education curriculum workers in a local situation if they were free to help develop the kind of curriculum needed for the local adult center or program. However, there are various "outside political forces" that come to play upon the local curriculum, and professional curriculum workers must be aware of them as they pursue improvement or developmental activities. These outside political forces are "outside" in the sense that they are not derived locally by curriculum workers and others in the local setting, and they are "political" in the sense that they will actually establish policy for the local curriculum design. As will be obvious there are numerous outside policy makers or political forces which have a very definite effect on the local adult curriculum regardless of local thinking. Thus, this major element of the curriculum is added for consideration by adult education curriculum workers and its impact will be viewed in detail. Briefly consider, for example, if a state department of education because of state legislation mandates that selected vocational areas or certain competencies must be found in the adult curriculum, then they must appear even though little value may be seen at the local level by professional adult education curriculum workers. Also, if an accrediting agency specifies selected areas to be taught and the local adult school wants to be accredited by that agency, then the school curriculum must conform to that regulation and actually accept the policy of the agency. Other factors, too, outside the realm of the adult education curriculum worker, as will be indicated, have a definite effect on the curriculum.

Three main forces--governmental agencies, private organizations, and interest groups--have varying degrees of influence on the policy of the local curriculum and in turn influence the curriculum in different ways. Therefore, this element or dimension must appear in a general curriculum model. This element which asks the question, "What outside forces actually play on the local curriculum?" is most important to consider when curriculum building occurs.

A representation of this element appears thus:

Outside Political Forces (What outside forces actually play on the local curriculum?)

> Governmental agencies
> Private agencies
> Interest groups

FIGURE 1.7 *Outside Political Forces*

It is suggested that this element should feed into
the general model between the rationale and goal elements because even though some apparent mandates about
the curriculum come from the outside, the rationale at
the outset of curriculum work can and should still be
specified locally for the local school. There still
appears to be adequate freedom for the local adult
program or school and its curriculum workers to go in
the direction that they deem important, and at the
same time handle various outside forces. But these
outside forces need to be considered before specifying
the goals for the education of adults in a school or
learning center because they too have a definite impact.

With the final element, outside political forces,
identified and defined the general curriculum model
appears on page 14.

As is obvious, the economic variable is absent
and, of course, is very important. In this day and
age the economics of schooling cannot be ignored and,
therefore, it is assumed that adult teachers and administrators and all curriculum workers are aware of
this factor and will give it consideration in all curriculum-building activities. Unfortunately, new curriculum ideas have to be tempered by the economics of
the situation; adult curriculum people must have this
ever present in their thinking.

This chapter has presented a brief introduction
and overview of a general model of a curriculum, its
elements, and structure. This was done to give a total
picture of the model and how the various elements of
it fit together in a coherent and consistent manner.
With this general curriculum model in mind the remainder

Rationale (What do we believe and feel about people, students, schooling, society, and other environmental phenomena and their meaning for an adult school program?)

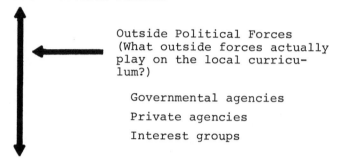

Psycho-Philosophical Factors

Sociocultural Factors

Outside Political Forces (What outside forces actually play on the local curriculum?)

Governmental agencies

Private agencies

Interest groups

Goals (What is worth learning in the adult view?)

General level   Cognitive domain

Intermediate level   Affective domain

Specific level   Psychomotor domain

Instructional Activities and Organization (How will the goals be accomplished?)

Instruction

Content Organization

Evaluation (Were the goals accomplished at three levels?)

General level goals

Intermediate level goals

Specific level goals

Internal means

External means

Formative data

Summative data

FIGURE 1.8 *General Curriculum Model*

of this volume will be devoted to deeper explication of the major elements in the model and its applicability to adult curriculum work. Chapter 2 looks at the concerns associated with the examination and statement of a curriculum rationale.

2 / Rationale

Rationale. The rationale for a curriculum, as suggested
earlier, provides a reason for a definite set of curriculum experiences. And, in turn, the curriculum
thrust or direction is a direct result of reviewing
carefully various concerns and issues in the socio-
logical-philosophical-psychological-cultural domains
of education. One must review and interpret these domains and their relationship to the adult student, the
school, the profession, and the total environment before proceeding to specify curriculum experiences.
After a close review and analysis a much clearer sense
of direction can be established for a curriculum design.

A rationale is not only a reason but actually a
defense or substantiation for proposing certain things
in the curriculum. In the day and age of accountability
all curriculum workers are forced to think critically
about the activities, goals, and experiences found in
the curriculum and must be ready to have a clear, concise reason for suggesting something. For example, if
an adult education center has an unusually large number of enrichment courses in its curriculum, there
should be definite reasons based on perhaps some careful analysis of psycho-philosophical concerns. Perhaps

the explicit expression of concern over individual differences and preferences of adults in the community
served and their desire for leading fuller and more
enriched lives might have been advanced as the reason.
Also, if an adult school has a rather extensive voca-
tional-occupational education program, the explicit
reason might have dealt with the sociocultural concerns
of the adult students with their individual need-dispositions and the desire to help them find a meaningful
and productive place in society. And, if an adult education school decides to develop a competency-based
curriculum it is hoped that the adult curriculum workers
in the situation have a sound, rational basis for doing
so, and not because a neighboring adult education center has one and it "seems to be doing alright."

The more carefully thought through the rationale
and the more explicit it is, the better the direction
will be for all curriculum decisions and following activities. To assist the adult curriculum worker in
decision making, two models will be advanced in the
areas of psychological-philosophical concerns and socio-
logical-cultural concerns to aid in reviewing critical
areas which have a direct bearing on the curriculum,
the adult student, and the professional adult educator.

Ever-present questions like "Why educate adults?"
"Education of adults for what purpose?" "What should
be taught to adults?" "What is my role in the educative
process?" "What impact does society have upon the adult
school and vice versa?" and many others constantly confront the curriculum worker. These questions must be
carefully reviewed and decisions made if we are to provide for educating adults for more successful living
in America. Decisions about these important concerns

will set some guides for curriculum experiences in
adult learning centers because how an individual feels,
believes, and interprets his environment and the people
in it will have an effect on his behavior as a professional person. The careful consideration of critical
factors will then lead to statements that can be translated into general goals and, in turn, curriculum
learning experiences.

PSYCHO-PHILOSOPHICAL CONCERNS

It is difficult, if not impossible, for one individual
to specify philosophical beliefs to which another person must adhere. But, all educators, and particularly
adult curriculum workers, must address their attention
to selected areas and make some critical decisions.
Some guides to major considerations will be presented
below which can assist in these critical decisions and
in the development of some consistent statements about
various beliefs. As a guide, Kneller[1] in his analysis
of educational philosophies suggests five areas for
consideration: metaphysics, human nature, epistemology,
values, and education. The following areas and model
although not inconsistent have been changed and modified for more direct use by the adult education curriculum worker.

Nature of Society. Since all people who attend adult
schools come from society, interact with it constantly,
and are expected to live successful lives in it during
and after completion of their schooling, some consideration as to the nature of our society and its implications for education is imperative for the adult

education curriculum person. Some questions have to be raised and answered by curriculum workers as they begin deliberation on the interrelationship of adult schooling and society.

What is society like? Is it dynamic, ever-changing? If so, what does this mean to the education of adults? Are values changing and/or relative? What are the values and beliefs of society? What impact do these values and beliefs have on the adult student and the adult school? Does society need improvement and/or refinement? If so, should the adult school become involved in the refinement and improvement processes? What does the transient and highly mobile nature of our society mean to the adult school? Can the adult school do something about the rapid technological advancements in society? What does unemployment and poverty mean to an adult center? Actually what is the relationship between society and adult education institutions? What other concerns and interpretations do curriculum people possess regarding society and what can or should adult schools and educational programs do about them? These and many other questions must be reviewed and suggestions developed before one can think about goals and an adult curriculum design.

Purposes of Adult Education. Another consideration would be to look at the basic purposes of educating adults in various educational settings. Perhaps few people would argue against the purpose that education should prepare and/or assist people to assume their position as happy, productive, decision-making members of our democratic society. However, ideas as to how to accomplish this and in turn organize the curriculum structure can vary quite significantly.

Should adult education deal only with the education of undereducated adults and focus basically on the literacy concept? Should adult education focus primarily on vocational efficiency? Should adult centers move toward lifelong learning for all adults? How much time and money should be spent on enrichment activities in adult education? Should the major effort of adult education be on underprivileged adults and making them self-sufficient people? Should adult educators think only of adult literacy and vocational efficiency or should they have concern for the total adult? Should adult education stress only selected competencies or feature some enrichment and leisure experiences? What role should adult education play in career orientation and placement? Should adult education concern itself with the social problems of adults or leave this to some other agency? What role should adult education play in the total life of all adults? What can adult education do to make life a better place for its clients, and should adult educators be concerned about continuous learning on the part of adults?

The purposes of adult education are obviously important to curriculum workers in adult education and must be carefully developed before they can specify any goals for the curriculum.

Nature of the Adult Learner. Making some interpretations and judgments about the nature of the adults who come to school for learning has a direct bearing on adult education curriculum workers as they think about the kinds of goals and experiences that should be designed for their clients. Do we see the adult learner as a rather passive individual who must be molded and shaped?

Or do we view the adult learner as an active, growing
being who interacts constantly with his environment?
Are adults uniquely different from one another? If they
are different, what does this mean for curriculum design work? What factors of a cultural nature play upon
the adult student and his learning? What are the values
and needs of adult learners, be they affluent or underprivileged? Should we be concerned about these values
and needs and other factors associated with the individual adult learner? Are we concerned about the individual dignity of each adult student? What are the
motivations of the adults who come for instruction in
adult classrooms? What psychological factors play upon
adults that can either hinder or enhance their desire
to learn? What effect does past performance in formal
schooling have on adult learners? What can adult curriculum workers do in overcoming these factors and
effects in building a meaningful curriculum for all
adults?

The adult learner with all of his personal ideas,
motivations, values, goals, beliefs--the individual
psychological makeup--must receive careful attention
by the adult education curriculum worker if the educative process is to be effective.

Learning Process. Another area that obviously has a direct bearing on curriculum work is how learning takes
place and for what purpose. Adult educators can and do
hold different beliefs about learning and the purpose
of it, which, of course, affects curriculum building
activities. Therefore, some careful thinking, inter-
pretation, and review must be done in this major area.

Is learning simply the acquisition of verified

knowledge with the utilization of this knowledge coming
later? Is it the successful completion of competencies
prescribed for adults? Or is learning an active ongoing
and experiencing process whereby what is being learned
has to have personal meaning to the learner? What is
the purpose of learning something? Is learning the
completion of selected tasks? Should competency be displayed at the end of a task to show that learning has
taken place? Should we have knowledge as an end or
should knowledge be a means to more knowledge? What
factors are involved in adults learning something? Do
these factors vary between adults? Should we be concerned with learning in the three behavioral domains--
cognitive, affective, and psychomotor? Is learning a
change in behavior? If so, how does behavior change in
adults? Can we as adult educators define what the outcomes of learning should be? Or should there be involvement by the adult clients themselves in this process?

Again, the careful thinking and examination of the
learning variable and its purpose should be a major
concern for adult curriculum workers before they begin
to develop any curriculum ideas. The impact of this
area on the curriculum is most significant.

Knowledge and the Curriculum. Another important philosophical area for the adult education curriculum worker to
consider deals with the purpose of knowledge and how
it shall be organized. What is the purpose of knowledge? Again, is it an end or a means to more knowledge? Can areas of knowledge be defined to which all
adult students must be exposed? Is there some necessary
knowledge for the good of all adults, a knowledge of
"most worth" concept? If not in all areas of the

curriculum, can we define necessary knowledge for selected areas? Should we define competencies for some or all adult students? Who defines them? What are these general and/or specific competencies? Will they guarantee successful performance in a given area of life? Are there other important uses of knowledge? How do we decide what should be taught?

How can we organize the knowledge variable? Should there be a logical, sequential order or should we consider psychological factors? Or can we combine both schools of thought? Should the curriculum be devoted to occupational, vocational, and other applicative areas, or can liberal, cultural, and aesthetic areas be interspersed for all adult students? Should the curriculum be elective or required? Should there be a problem-solving orientation to the curriculum? Should it be competency-based? If so, why? Should there be a very definite list of behavioral and/or performance objectives that should be achieved by all adult students at various levels? Finally, should one area of study, because of its uniqueness, be organized differently from another for better teaching and learning?

Viewing the purpose of knowledge, its organization, and use is critical for adult education curriculum workers. They must make judgments after very careful examination and thought because this strikes at the heart of curriculum work.

Role of the Professional. A final concern to which adult curriculum workers (all adult educators) should address their attention is their role in the classroom, in the adult center or school, in the profession, and in society. How a person judges one's place as a classroom

and school professional in the total educative process
is important because different role perceptions will
cause different behaviors to exist and thus different
end products on the part of the curriculum and adult
students. Should the adult teacher and/or administrator
play an active role in curriculum development and
improvement activities? If so, what kind of role?
Should the local curriculum worker make the decisions
as to what should be taught and how to teach it? Should
the professional involve others in deciding curriculum
philosophy, goals, and directions? What role should the
adult educator play in controversial issues in the
curriculum?

Should adult educators' concern be for subject matter only or should the total welfare and development
of the adult client be of concern to them? What kinds
of professional behavior (that is, democratic, auto-
cratic) should prevail, not only in teaching and curriculum work but in all professional activities? Since
there is a high incidence of part-time teachers and
administrators in adult education, what role should
these people play in the total process? How do adult
educators see their own self-improvement and personal
staff development efforts? Are adult educators keeping
up to date so as to do a more effective and professional
job? Finally, what role should the professional adult
educator play in political and legislative activities
that pertain to the welfare of adult education in
general?

The above six philosophical areas are arbitrary on
the part of the writer but should serve the purpose of
causing adult education curriculum workers to think
seriously about the "reasons" for educating all adults

in their centers and about developing curriculum experiences for them. The brief review and example questions in each category above only scratch the surface; they are only a beginning. However, these and many more like them must be considered and reviewed before any significant curriculum design work can begin. Without careful thinking in these areas, the curriculum has little if any base on which to be developed. There will be no position or rationale for developing any curriculum experiences.

Combining these major factors into a model for analysis and, in turn, for decision making would result in the diagrammatic expression found in Figure 2.1, as shown on page 26.

The model suggests that curriculum workers take the six major areas of concern and pass them through their perceptual screen and then make some judgments on what adult education should be and why. The perceptual screen is, of course, the individual's own view of his/her environment and the objects, events and people in it. The screen is a result of living, learning, and interacting and is made up of the person's values, experiences, attitudes, beliefs, needs, and self-experiences. Each individual probably possesses a different screen than others and thus should think carefully and be ready to support his/her own beliefs and judgments. This is the first step in effective rationale building. Also, it behooves all critical adult education curriculum workers to re-examine continuously their beliefs because of new information received through readings, discussions, personal staff development activities, and added

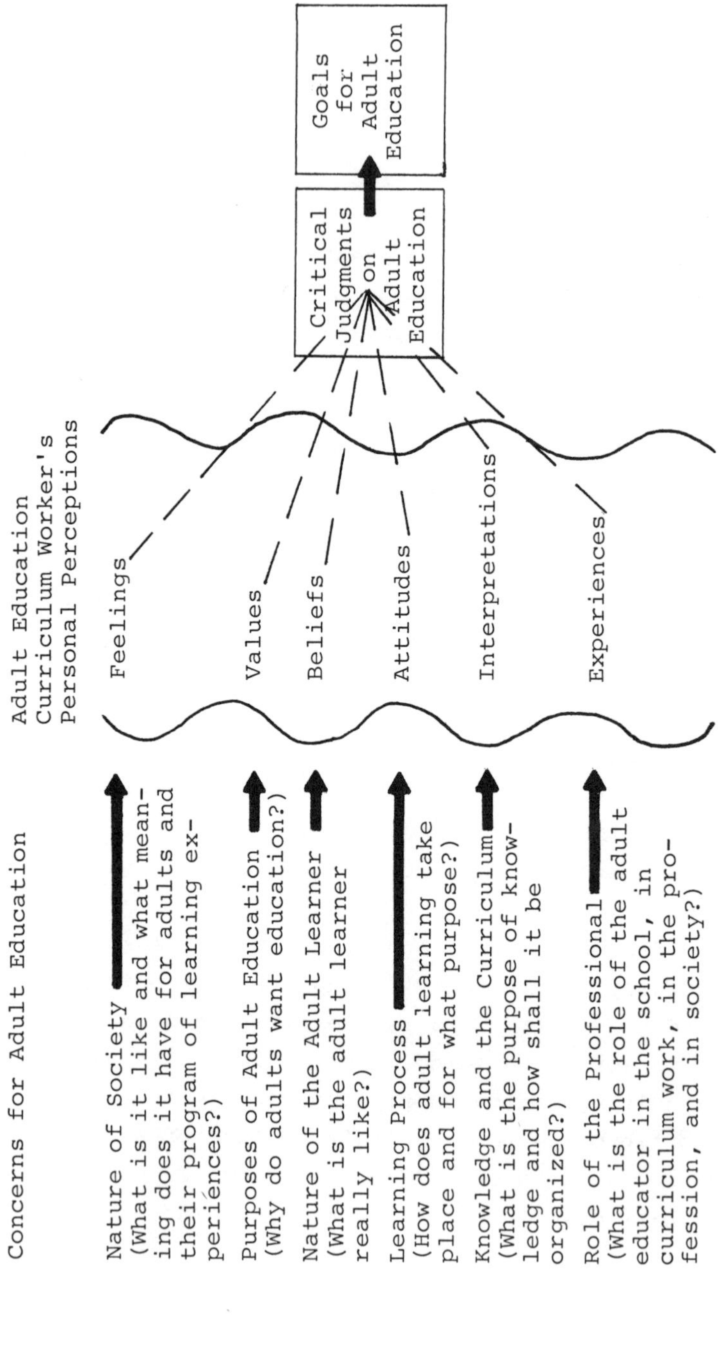

Concerns for Adult Education

Nature of Society
(What is it like and what meaning does it have for adults and their program of learning experiences?)

Purposes of Adult Education
(Why do adults want education?)

Nature of the Adult Learner
(What is the adult learner really like?)

Learning Process
(How does adult learning take place and for what purpose?)

Knowledge and the Curriculum
(What is the purpose of knowledge and how shall it be organized?)

Role of the Professional
(What is the role of the adult educator in the school, in curriculum work, in the profession, and in society?)

Adult Education
Curriculum Worker's
Personal Perceptions

Feelings

Values

Beliefs

Attitudes

Interpretations

Experiences

Critical Judgments on Adult Education

Goals for Adult Education

FIGURE 2.1 *Psycho-philosophical Concerns for Adult Education*

experiences. If we believe that change is present, then
we must keep abreast of it.

SOCIOCULTURAL CONCERNS

Before the curriculum worker can make some critical
judgments on education in the form of a rationale, it
may be advisable to view the various sociological-
anthropological variables that come into play and that
affect the curriculum, the adult student in his environment, and the professional adult educator. Viewing
concerns in this domain will provide more personal and
professional awareness and, therefore, lend more precision to the entire curriculum-building process.

Consideration for sociocultural factors that
surround each adult student in an educational setting
is critical since these factors affect his/her behavior and learning potential. The beliefs and values of
the dominant culture, the personal need dispositions
of each adult learner influenced by a subculture, and
the interplay of role and personality in a classroom
are some variables that need explanation and clarifi-
cation for the adult education curriculum worker.
Further, a relationship of the important variables in
a social system and the resulting goal behavior must
be made explicit for analysis and, in turn, for tying
in together with psycho-philosophical factors for a
concise statement of a curriculum rationale.

An analytic model that helps explain, relate, and
clarify the variable in a social system was developed
by Getzels and Thelen[2] and later modified by Getzels.[3]
This model begins with a social system which in the
case of adult education is generally the community.

Within the social system two major dimensions are
present--the sociological or normative and the psychological or individual. At the normative level a social
system has institutions (adult schools and centers in
this case) which require certain roles to be played.
The roles in turn are seen more analytically as what
expectations the role incumbent is required to display.
The role-expectations really define what should occur
in an institution and thus lead to goal behavior of
the institution. The institution is in fact defined
and does suggest that certain roles and expectations
are necessary for the fulfillment of the goals of the
social system. The first dimension may be represented
as follows:

Social system $\longrightarrow$ Institution $\longrightarrow$ Role $\longrightarrow$ Expectations $\longrightarrow$
Institutional Goal-behavior

In other words this dimension reflects the fact that
social systems such as communities define institutions
like an adult school or even an adult program to achieve
certain goals for the good of the community. Again,
this is done by defining certain roles that should be
played which in turn can be more precisely viewed by
the expectations of the institution. When expectations
are fulfilled, institutional goals should be achieved
for the good of the social system.

However, since a social system (community) also
contains individuals who possess certain personalities
and need-dispositions, the second or individual dimension comes into being. This is to say that the individual dimension, running parallel to the normative,

has individuals (adult students) with distinct personalities which are reflected more precisely in the need-
dispositions of each individual. These all lead to
individual goal-behavior. This individual dimension
may be represented thus:

Social → Individuals → Personalities → Need- →
system   dispositions

Individual Goal-behavior

This dimension suggests that social systems are com-
prised of individuals who have distinct personalities
which are more closely viewed by the need-dispositions
of the individuals. And these individuals with their
unique personalities and need-dispositions have individual goals which are important to them.

Bringing together the behavioral aspects of the
individual and the role expectations of the institution
will provide a means of understanding the behavior and
interactions of specific adult clients in an adult
institution. A graphic representation of these two
dimensions in a social system and the resulting goal-
behavior is as follows:

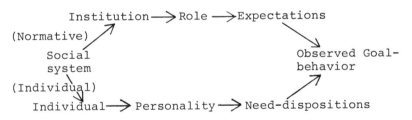

FIGURE 2.2 *Normative and Individual Dimensions*

These two dimensions of a social system, as might be expected, do not operate in a cultural vacuum so additional variables at the anthropological level can be identified and thus come into play. Each institution, or in this case the adult program or school, is embedded in a culture that possesses certain beliefs and characteristics (ethos) which in turn are displayed in a set of values or a value system held by that culture. All of these factors play upon the adult school because, in a way, they specify what is expected of the institution. The same case can be built for the individual because the adult, too, is embedded in a culture, perhaps subculture, because of his/her family, personal relationships, friends, job, neighborhood, and other peer groups. The adult student's culture has a certain ethos which displays a value system, and these factors play upon the adult's need-dispositions and individual goals. Because of the significant reciprocal influence of the culture with its ethos and values upon the institution and individual, this anthropological level is added to the basic model. It now appears in Figure 2.3, as shown on page 31.

Because of the inherent differences in the two dimensions of the social system, there could be conflicts and deviant perceptions between the individual adult student with his/her personality and need-dispositions and the adult institution with its role and expectations. This model handles this concern with the identification of a group to serve as a buffer between the institution and the individual. The group, which mediates the institutional requirements and the individual dispositions, actually imposes a balance between

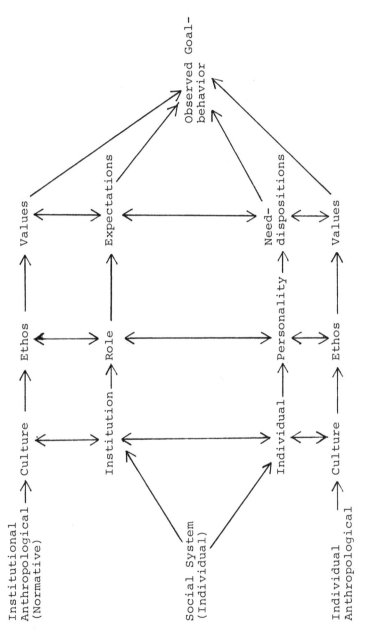

FIGURE 2.3 *Normative and Individual Dimensions with Cultural Influences*

the two and helps to support the institution when certain roles and expectations seem important, and to
support when necessary the individual adult student
when he/she expresses his/her idiosyncratic personality
and need-dispositions. This is done by the group's
fostering a climate and definite intentions. The final
dimension of the model would be diagrammatically represented as follows:

Social
system $\longrightarrow$ Group $\longrightarrow$ Climate $\longrightarrow$ Intentions $\longrightarrow$ Goal-behavior

The group-climate dimension completes the model and is
essential for the effective functioning of an adult
student in an adult educational institution.

A graphic representation of the complete model
including the group-climate-intentions dimension is
shown on page 33.

In viewing the entire model, it can be noted that
each stratum relates directly to the adult school and
the work of the adult education curriculum person.
Interpreted broadly the institution-role-expectation
stratum (B) in this case is the curriculum of the
school. This is reflected directly in the learning experiences of the school because it specifies what is
expected for the adult student to attain goal-behavior
as prescribed by the school. The institutional-anthropological level (A) is the dominant culture with its
beliefs and values, and in most cases would reflect
the middle-class culture. The reciprocal influence
here would thus indicate that generally the curriculum
of adult schools would reflect a middle-class value
system.

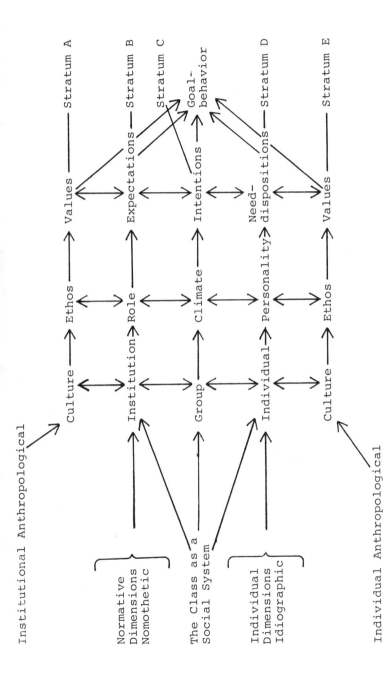

FIGURE 2.4 *Complete Model for Analysis of a Social System and Goal-behavior*[4]

On the other hand, the individual-personality-need-dispositions stratum (D) represents each individual adult student who makes up a school or class. The individual-anthropological stratum (E) represents the cultural "package" that each individual adult student possesses and brings to school and class each time and could reflect any subcultural value system.

Finally, the group-climate-intentions level (C) for all intense and purposes is the professional adult educator because he/she is the one who leads the group and fosters the desirable learning climate through work with adult students.

The Getzels model lends precision to the adult education curriculum worker's job as it brings to the level of awareness some of the conditions and variables that surround the adult school, the adult student, and the curriculum, and will identify the mediating variables for the curriculum worker to use in the sound decision-making process.

It will assist adult education curriculum people in defining reasons for the curriculum experiences for adult clients who come from differing subcultures. It will cause them to look carefully at expectations for all adult students in a school setting. And, it will clearly identify their role in not only curriculum building, but in teaching and administering experiences for adults because it actually identifies what is present in a sociocultural system and provides some direction as to what must be done to cope with the problems. This, of course, is a definite aid to goal statements and curriculum designs.

To aid in the development of a more precise statement for a rationale for a curriculum, the adult education curriculum worker may utilize together the Getzels model and the six-point model (p. 26) in the psycho-philosophical area to lend more analysis and synthesis and, in turn, critical judgments. The institutional-anthropological stratum (A) in the Getzels model can assist in thinking about the Nature of Society; the individual-anthropological (E) and the individual (D) strata help with the Nature of the Learner category; the institutional stratum (B) can provide some additional assistance for thinking about the Knowledge and Curriculum and Purposes of Education areas; and the Group-Climate-Intentions dimension (C) can assist curriculum workers in thinking about their Role as Professionals.

With some very careful analysis and thinking by adult education curriculum workers in this important area, some solid ideas will emerge which can serve as a reason for the suggested curriculum experiences. These ideas can be put on paper in the form of a curriculum rationale utilizing the Six-point psycho-philosophical model. Carefully thought-through statements can be made under each major heading outlining the beliefs and feelings regarding the general direction that a curriculum or program might take and the reasons for that direction. This should be an open document operating at the general level, but should give a real sense of direction and meaning to all learning experiences. It should not be cast in bronze, but firm enough in terms of ideas and beliefs to support the reasoning for adult education in a given center, school, or program.

Adult curriculum workers, in displaying sound professional behavior, must assess continuously the reasoning (rationale) for curriculum experiences because needs, values, persuasions, and perceptions change. These changes occur because new knowledge, information, ideas, research, and thinking emerge, and society itself changes creating new areas of concern for curriculum people. If the desire to provide the best possible experiences for adult clients is expressed, then adult education curriculum workers must continuously reexamine issues and concerns confronting them, society, and the educative process in general. Therefore, curriculum workers must keep abreast of ideas and events through reading, thinking, discussion, staff development, and actual interaction with their environment.

Finally, in thinking about and drafting a rationale for curriculum experiences, the adult education professional might entertain three concerns. First, there should be consistency and coherence among the judgments and beliefs between each category. In other words, if curriculum workers feel that one of the purposes of adult education is the development of life-oriented problem-solving abilities, their views on learning, the use of knowledge, and the role of the teacher should reflect this. It is important to search for order and consistency when adult curriculum people specify how they feel and believe philosophically about education.

Secondly, and perhaps more important, is the necessity of translating beliefs and judgments into goals that can actually be placed into a curriculum so that the desirable behavior can be developed on the part of the adult students. For example, if curriculum workers see the adult student as an active, interacting social being and that learning is an active, ongoing process

of inquiry, this should be reflected in the goals and
curriculum design and carried out at the experience
level. The curriculum design would then be so structured
as to encourage inquiry, thinking, and activity.

Thirdly, professional adult curriculum workers,
both teachers and administrators, should consider the
opinions, beliefs, and judgments of their adult clients
and the community membership in which the educators
carry on their work. Since adult schools are designed
to serve adult members of a given community or area,
numerous members of the community should have a say in
the expression of what their adult education program
should be. This is part of the democratic process, and
it seems logical for community members to make their
feelings known at this general, abstract level and
perhaps at the general level of goal statements to be
discussed later. This does not necessarily mean that
only lay opinion will be utilized; it means that all
involved should be heard. Of course, professional adult
curriculum workers must themselves think carefully
about all rationale factors so as to provide leadership
and insure that something of importance has received
consideration. Perhaps only professional adult educators
can do this.

Once careful thinking about society, adult clients,
knowledge, schooling, and other important areas has
been completed, the next move is to translate these
beliefs into a curriculum design and more specifically
goal statements. However, before this process can take
place, it appears important for adult curriculum workers
to look at the outside forces that play upon the local
adult curriculum. These outside forces actually establish policy for an adult center's curriculum and,

therefore, must be brought to the attention of curriculum people. Chapter 3 looks at outside political forces
and their effect on the local adult curriculum.

3 / Outside Political Forces

Decisions about what actually appears in a curriculum
are made by a variety of individual people and groups.
These decisions are in essence statements of policy
as to what should or should not be taught within a
local adult educational institution. Many of the policy statements are derived from within the local
center and organization, where perhaps many would argue they should be, but some emerge because of "outside
influence." These outside influences do establish policy and thus are political forces; therefore, they
must be brought to the attention of local adult education curriculum workers because of their impact on
their curriculum. Awareness of these outside forces
should help adult educators make more intelligent decisions regarding the curriculum for their adult
clients.

In regard to public school curriculum making, Kirst
and Walker state:

Since local districts have ultimate authority and re-
sponsibility for carrying out curriculum policy, and
much authority for determining it, we focus our attention on the curriculum decisions of local schools and
the activities of individuals and groups in local school
systems as they engage in these collective decisions.

Inevitably this focus draws us into a consideration of the state, regional and national factors--governmental and private--that condition and constrain local decision makers.[1]

Many outside factors which do, in fact, put certain conditions and constraints on local decision making by curriculum workers are found also within the domain of adult education and therefore must be brought to the attention of adult education curriculum workers and must be given serious consideration. Awareness that these forces and factors are present and that they do affect curriculum policy is the critical concern. However, as will be noted, the local adult curriculum worker perhaps has more control over outside influences than readily meets the eye, but the forces are present and must be identified and discussed before proceeding to the goal statement element.

It appears that curriculum people in general have long ignored outside policy makers in their discussion and thinking about curriculum development activities. Mention is given to outside influences and then they are passed over lightly, as if they do not do much or as if little can be done about them. Or, perhaps curriculum workers have just accepted them as a necessary evil and taken their influences for granted. Preoccupation with local control and improvement of the local curriculum has perhaps created this situation. However, as is noted by the work of Kirst and Walker,[2] outside policy influences are many and varied, strong and subtle, and, in fact, can have quite an impact on local curriculum work. These influences should be identified and their impact seen so that adult curriculum workers can lend more precision to their curriculum building efforts.

The policy-making influence structure outside the local educational institution is a complex one with different forces playing upon the institution in different ways. Even with the complexities present, certain types of influence can be identified and explained.

Outside Policy Makers. Kirst and Walker suggest that policy makers outside the domain of the local education agency actually fall into three main categories. These three major groups, governmental agencies, private organizations, and various interest groups, as will be noted have varying influences on the curriculum.

Within the governmental agency category the three usual levels of federal, state, and local are identified. In most cases the state level is where considerable policy making takes place. This comes generally from legislative mandates and the rules and regulations of the state departments governing adult education. The federal level, in delegating much of the educational authority to states, has little impact in terms of what should or should not appear in a local adult curriculum. However, in many federally sponsored programs in adult education numerous rules and regulations are advanced by the federal government which must be adhered to by the local adult education agency. Even though there is no national curriculum for all of the many adult education programs in this country, as appears in some other countries throughout the world, considerable regulation and control are exercised by the federal government in the execution of the programs. Local governments (mayors, city councils, and

so forth) too have less impact than state governments
on curriculum policy making, but do exert some influence especially in very large cities and in certain
programs such as those supported by the Comprehensive
Employment and Training Act (CETA) and which are sponsored by the federal government but directed generally
by noneducation agencies such as city or county governments.

Examples of the many private organizations which
influence local adult curriculum policy making would
include ones like foundations (Mott, Kellogg), accrediting agencies (North Central Association for separately administered adult programs), testing companies
(American Council on Education with its GED), and the
numerous textbook companies that develop and publish
adult education materials. The influence from these
organizations, as will be noted, is varied and sometimes subtle.

Finally, several interest groups can influence the
local curriculum in various ways. Examples could include ethnic organizations such as the NAACP and His-
panic and American Indian groups, some labor unions,
the National Association of Manufacturers, and some
gerontology groups. These interest groups are not
normally concerned with adult education solely, but
will jump into the educational arena when they deem it
important to their clientele. These large national
groups have the machinery and money to bring influence
to the adult education community and do so on occasion.

A brief representation of this element of the curriculum is as follows:

Outside Political Forces

        Governmental
          Local
          State
          Federal

        Private Organizations
          E.g.: Foundations
                Accrediting Agencies
                Testing Agencies
                Textbook Companies

        Interest Groups
          E.g.: NAACP
                NAM
                AFL-CIO

FIGURE 3.1 *Outside Curriculum Policy Makers*

It should be obvious to the reader at this point that considerable influence on the curriculum is exerted at the local level by other groups and individuals than just the local professional adult educators. Advisory committees, boards of education, boards of trustees, professional staff members, and other citizens and groups of citizens locally have an impact on the curriculum offerings in an adult education program, school, or center. This is assumed within this present text, and, of course, these groups and individuals will be involved in various capacities within the "local determination" concept of curriculum building. Only "outside" influences of a national, state, and regional nature are reviewed in this writing effort.

Three Ways of Affecting Curriculum Policy Making. In their analysis of curriculum policy making Kirst and Walker "distinguish three ways in which national or regional agencies affect state and local curriculum policy making: by establishing minimum standards, by generating curriculum alternatives, and by demanding curriculum change."[3] The above-identified groups, agencies or organizations, of course, can influence curriculum policy at the local level in more than one way, as will be seen upon examination of the three major ways in which the influence takes place.

In the first case of groups or organizations establishing minimum curriculum standards, it is interesting to note that there is no national governmental minimum standard recommended in most adult programs. This is the result perhaps of an emphasized "local control" concept, the delegation of authority to the states, and the fear of a national curriculum. However, great similarities exist throughout the nation in many adult education programs and this might be attributed to various national nongovernmental agencies that actually demand a minimum national curriculum standard below which most adult institutions would not like to fall. Private accrediting agencies are one of the identified major influences in this area as they in essence dictate many standards of a curriculum nature to which a school or program must adhere or lose accreditation by the given agency. And, since school people in general fear the loss of accreditation, the various agencies have a great influence over the curriculum offerings in a school or program at most levels and in different individual areas. If applicable to a given adult program, adult education curriculum workers should become apprised of the various standards that private accrediting agencies set for programs and schools. Generally these standards are perceived as minimal by curriculum people, but the standards must still receive attention.

Testing agencies are another outside influence which has a standardizing effect on the curriculum. To emphasize this point in adult education, over 700,000 people take the General Educational Development (GED) test yearly, and numerous organizations require the successful completion of it for continued education, training, or work opportunities. Consequently, local adult schools and programs which teach in adult basic education and offer preparatory work for passing the GED have little choice as to what subject areas are emphasized in that particular program. A GED preparatory program will emphasize work in writing skills, social studies, science, reading skills, and mathematics because fifty state departments of education, the District of Columbia, six United States territories or possessions, and most Canadian provinces and territories now use the GED tests as the basis for issuance of high school equivalency credentials. The same effect can be seen in the utilization of tests for licensing of selected occupations or professions (for example, nursing) in many states and territories. The determination of the precise content in many of these areas is pretty much a foregone conclusion since generally local adult schools and programs not only want to look good, but have their students do well on these standardized and other tests. Adult education curriculum workers are literally forced into apprising themselves of the nature of the tests and the content emphasized.

Another identified major influence on the curriculum of a local adult school or program comes from state departments of education. The state departments may not only mandate minimum standards but specify certain courses, textbooks, and amounts of time spent in selected content areas. Since the state departments have this measure of regulatory control over standards through legislation and/or statutes and delegation by the federal government and in turn provide state and federal financial support for local programs, the schools will generally follow the prescribed standards.

State departments or other state agencies generally set the standards for acceptably passing the GED test. They set requirements and standards for licensing and certification of selected personnel. And, they might through legislation require that certain competencies be met and that certain courses (for example, consumer education) be found in certain programs. Some of the selected requirements and standards may be unique to a particular state. For example, adults must pass a United States and State Constitution test in Illinois in addition to the GED before receiving the high school equivalency certificate in that state. In the case of any requirements for any state, local adult administrators and curriculum workers have little alternative but to see that the various requirements and standards are, in fact, reflected in the local adult curriculum offerings. And since state (and federal through the state) aid is significant in terms of dollars and cents and required for program maintenance, the reason for incorporating requirements and standards appears to be doubly important. Again, adult education curriculum builders must be aware of state and federal requirements

and standards as they foster curriculum experiences
for their adult clients. Upon the careful review of
the various state and federal requirements by local
adult curriculum workers, they might surprisingly find
that considerable flexibility does, however, exist to
meet those requirements.

Finally, in this general area it is suggested that
teaching and other professional associations can have
an influence on what would be taught in a curriculum
of a local adult education center. Some associations
have rather broad interests in adult and continuing
education such as the National Association for Public
Continuing and Adult Education, the Adult Education
Association of the U.S.A., the National University
Extension Association, and the National Community Education Association. Others such as the American Management Association, the American Vocational Association, and the American Nurses' Association focus on
more specific areas within the general adult curriculum.
Many of these national and state affiliated associations
can bring pressure to bear in selected areas to ensure
that these areas are represented in the curriculum.
Alert adult education curriculum workers should keep
themselves apprised of the philosophy, thinking, and
efforts brought forth by the professional associations
involved in adult education and review the implications
for the particular curriculum work at hand.

In terms of alternative generators and their effect on the curriculum, a variety of possibilities
emerges. While many curriculum decisions at the local
level are affected by the broad category of minimum
standards, other outside agencies can provide a variety

of curricular and instructional alternatives from which selections can be made, and which in turn can influence the curriculum of an adult program or school. Even though great flexibility exists in being able to make a decision on an alternative at the local level, the decision is still limited in the fact that alternatives may be limited (based on local perceptions), and when an alternative is selected, policy from the outside is actually established in the local curriculum. Perhaps the biggest of alternative generators is the textbook and curriculum materials industry.

Local educational institutions of all kinds rely very heavily on commercial textbooks and curriculum materials for instruction because of their general inability to produce their own. Also, textbooks and associated materials are used extensively in many individual classrooms. Because of these facts, textbook authors and publishers have a great deal to say about what appears in the local curriculum. If, for example, adult curriculum workers decide on reading materials for their adult basic education classes which come from Publisher A, instead of Publishers B or C, they in essence are accepting many of the policies, goals, strategies, evaluation techniques, and ideas of Publisher A for this part of their curriculum. This can happen in all areas of the curriculum where outside materials are used in the instructional process. Therefore, substantial curriculum influence does exist even though a free choice after a careful examination was made by local curriculum people. It should be kept in mind, though, that the individual adult teachers have and do exert considerable freedom in the use of commercial materials in their individual instructional situations.

The federal government with its considerable resources and defined agencies and organizations like the Department of Health, Education and Welfare, the National Institute of Education, the National Institutes of Health, the Office of Education, and the National Science Foundation is another alternative generator for adult curriculum influence policy making. The Adult Performance Level (APL) study is a prime example of defining an alternative program for basic literacy for adults. The curriculum development work in the five competency areas of functional literacy provides a viable alternative to the more traditional instructional methods of teaching undereducated adults. The CETA program, mentioned above, is another example of federal involvement in program alternatives for adult education. Actually, Section 309 (now 310) of the federal Adult Education Act provides funds specifically for the development of innovative practices (alternatives) for use in adult basic education. The federal government, therefore, can and does provide resources for program development in selected areas of adult education which definitely alters ways of providing instruction for adults. And, the fact that the government and its agencies have become involved in certain areas of the adult curriculum and not in others further indicates its influence in curriculum policy making for adult education.

Private foundations have also provided leadership in the development of alternative ways of operating

and thinking in adult education. The Mott Foundation
with its considerable efforts in community education
and the Kellogg Foundation with its efforts in continuing education and extension work are examples of
private foundations that have influenced adult education by offering different alternatives to the solu-
tions of certain problems confronting adults.

Within this category are found professional associations and college and university professors as two
other major alternative generators. Individual associations and professions, as mentioned above, even
with less financial resources, have had an impact on
curriculum offerings in a variety of adult programs.
Professors through their writing, speaking, teaching,
and consulting can generate alternative ways of educating adults and thus bring some influence to local
curriculum building efforts.

Finally, it should be noted that professional
adult educators, teachers, supervisors, and administrators, through their writings and personal interaction at conferences, workshops, and associational
meetings have generated other alternatives for consideration by the local decision makers. The alternatives proposed by these professional adult educators
tend to deal with specific rather than general principles and ideas. The interchange between and among
these professional adult educators is an effective
means of getting alternative ideas into the curriculum.
After all if some alternative way of working with
adults works in one local situation, it just might
work in another.

It is emphasized again that when local adult curriculum workers exercise their option to select outside

alternatives in the form of books, curriculum materials, and even programs for use in their local curriculum, they are also accepting much of the goals, philosophy, and policy of the alternatives. This may not be wrong, but it emphasizes the fact that it is important to check carefully that the outside alternatives that are utilized or proposed for utilization fit in with and are consistent with the expressed philosophy, goals, and policies of the local adult education institution. Severe incongruities might occur in the total program offerings of the institution if consistency and compatibility are not present.

The final way in which agencies and groups can influence adult education curriculum policy is through a process of demanding change. Instead of generating alternative schemes to curriculum planning and innovation, some groups can decide on one and give firm support to it, or they can define a special interest area for adult education and bring sufficient influence to see to it that it receives attention in an adult education institution's program of learning. Considerable pressure can be brought to bear on adult education in general by various organizations and groups. Groups representing unions, business, ethnic organizations, and older Americans can exert substantial influence nationally, regionally, and locally on adult education curriculum policy, but generally not in the normal policy-making sense. They just demand that certain considerations be given to their ideas. Again, these groups generally are not normally interested in adult education solely, but can and will bring influence on educational processes when it is deemed important.

Many times the influence comes in rather crisis-oriented situations like wars, racial disturbances, unemployment, and recessions. These situations tend to cause groups to look to education for immediate help to solve various social problems. The crisis-oriented influence on curriculum policy making is perhaps not the best approach for sound decisions, but it is present and adult curriculum workers must be aware of it. And, since crises seem to appear so frequently in American society, crisis policy making may be the rule instead of the exception. In any case because of this phenomenon, such groups can exert pressure and demand that change (or in some instances that no change) takes place in adult education curriculum offerings.

The above discussion again does not look at local interest or influences that can play upon the curriculum offerings. It is assumed that critical adult education curriculum workers will ascertain the ideas, interests, and perceptions of their immediate clientele, both adult students and other community members, as they begin any assessment and developmental activities. The channels for local concern should always be open, and the comments received should be given very careful consideration.

Viewing the outside forces or factors that play upon the local decision-making process of an adult education institution is of great importance to the curriculum worker. It might be argued that, with the exception of state departments of education and licensing, other licensing agencies, and federal laws and requirements, local curriculum people have mostly complete control over these outside forces. But perhaps this is not the case. If an adult school or program wants to play the accreditation "game" (have full accreditation), it will have to play by accreditation "rules." If an adult institution wants "good" achievement for its adult clients as measured by a national norm of some sort, it will have to see that the appropriate learning experiences to fulfill the testing measures are found in the curriculum. And, if a local school desires the use of "outside" funds to finance various special projects, chances are it will have to accept the guidelines (policy) of the funding agency in its implementation.

In some ways the same case can be made for the alternative generator category. For example, if an adult school desires more competency-based activity in its curriculum, chances are curriculum workers will select the alternative curriculum package and/or books that stress this instructional process. But as they do, they will accept much of the philosophy, goals, instruction, and evaluation associated with the alternative. Modifications can and do occur but the main theme (policy) is still present.

Upon reviewing carefully the outside mandates, requirements, and ideas that are "foisted" on adult curriculum workers, it might be seen that many deal with specific areas to be covered in a program. Considerable freedom is still available to adult education curriculum people to suggest resulting behaviors (goals), instructional strategies, and evaluation techniques. In other words, curriculum workers can meet many outside requirements and still do what they feel is important for their adult clients in their institutions based on their philosophical expressions (curriculum rationale).

By combining into one model the above-identified outside forces and factors and the ways in which they can cause influence on an adult education curriculum, a graphic representation of this important area and its relationship to the curriculum rationale and goals would appear thus:

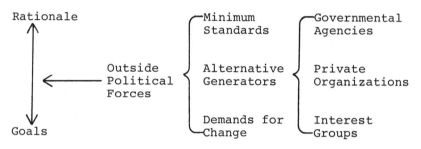

FIGURE 3.2 *Outside Political Forces*

From the above structure it can be seen that certain forces outside the local adult educational organization can establish minimum standards, generate alternatives and/or demand changes that can result in definite policies for a local curriculum. These policies then filter into the actual curriculum design starting with the goals of the curriculum. The forces without a doubt have an impact on the development of a rationale because consideration will be given to them as adult educators review their thinking about society, students, purposes of education, knowledge, and so forth. But a pure curriculum rationale can and should be developed first by specifying certain beliefs, values, and persuasions about the worth of adults and adult schooling and then consideration can be given to outside forces. In this manner a philosophical base is established to guide all curriculum building activity from there on. After that, outside forces must receive attention before the actual design of the curriculum is established. Thus the political forces arrow feeds into the model between the rationale and goals.

Again, it should be kept in mind that the local adult education curriculum workers and others have considerable flexibility and freedom even with some of these outside constraints placed on them. These outside forces must, however, be considered in adult curriculum work and must be weighed along with other factors like finances (economic variable), school populations, facilities, and others as adult educators begin development and improvement activities.

Upon making many of these considerations known, the next step in curriculum building is the actual curriculum design beginning with appropriate goal statements. The next chapter gives attention to the goals and objectives for the adult education institution's curriculum and for instruction.

4 / Curriculum Goals

Upon the productive thinking about a curriculum rationale and the development of it and upon the careful consideration of outside policy forces that play upon a local adult learning program, the adult education curriculum worker's next concern rests with the definition of goals for the curriculum and for the instructional program. These three major elements (rationale, outside forces, and goals) come into play together and must be in harmony to have a consistent and coherent set of curriculum statements, but the goals themselves actually set the stage for the curriculum design itself. All activities, materials, and experiences to which adult students are exposed are contingent upon the goals expressed for the curriculum. And, since all evaluation measures should be geared directly to goal statements, the goals are of utmost importance for the curriculum and should be treated as such. Mager makes this point cogently by stating:

When clearly defined goals are lacking, it is impossible to evaluate a course or program efficiently, and there is no sound basis for selecting appropriate materials, content, or instructional methods. After all, the machinist does not select a tool until he knows what operation he intends to perform. Neither does a composer orchestrate a score until he knows what effects he wishes to achieve. Similarly, a builder does not select his materials or specify a schedule for construction until he has his blueprints (objectives) before him.[1]

Therefore, the definition of goals to guide further curriculum work is important and must receive critical attention at this point.

Because of the broad nature of curriculum offerings in adult centers and schools and the many activities that fall within these offerings, some method of organizing goal statements for all kinds of curriculum and instructional activities is imperative. Krathwohl[2] advances a model on goal statements that suggests that educational objectives should be stated at three levels of specificity, corresponding to the three phases of development of instruction. This three-level model is most effective for curriculum building and lends precision to the adult curriculum worker's activities.

The first level is the most general level and is used primarily for program planning at the broad and abstract level. This involves the statement of goals and areas of study for an entire program covering several years of education within a school or center. Such a statement of goals at the general level might be developed for a vocational program, a continuous training program, or an adult basic education program. These general statements of goals serve to guide and direct curriculum efforts over longer segments of an adult student's program. The second level, the intermediate level, is more concrete and is designed for curriculum development for an instructional course or module of study. More precise statements of goals are included at this level to govern the instructional efforts for more specific packages of instruction such as an individual unit on welding in the vocational program, a semester course on improving reading skills in an Adult Basic Education (ABE) program, a class on indoor plants, investments for the woman, or keeping physically fit in an enrichment program, and a course on improving sales in a major business. The third level, the most specific level, is geared toward instructional material building and focuses on specific lesson plans and sequencing of specific goals. These very precise statements guide and direct the day-to-day behavioral change on the part of adult students.

These three levels appear extremely important in goals stating even though an adult educator's primary concern might seem to rest with the specific level in the classroom. For the adult education curriculum worker all three levels are critical in order to develop a coherent set of experiences for all adult students over varying periods of schooling. And the levels are important for the analysis of the entire instructional program of the adult school because as Krathwohl suggests:

1. Each level of analysis permits the development of the next more specific level.

2. Mastery objectives can be analyzed to greater specificity than transfer objectives.

3. Curricula gain adoption by consensus that what is taught is of value. Consensus is more easily gained at the more abstract levels of analysis.

4. There are usually several alternative ways of analyzing objectives at the most specific level. Objectives at the more abstract level provide a referent for evaluating these alternatives.[3]

In other words this three-level model offers many advantages to the adult curriculum worker for more precise curriculum building. It permits the definition of general program goals through a consensus of all appropriate decision makers. This definition of goals at the general level is important for direction giving and can be reached with less difficulty if values are expressed in broad, general terms; consensus on what the programs should be doing can be reached more easily when operating at this level. With the definition of goals at this level, curriculum workers can build more precise and measurable (if necessary) goals for various instructional units of study. The general level of goals serves as a constant referent to insure that the other levels are in consonance with it. And in doing this, it gives professional adult teachers the freedom to pursue more specific objectives (goals) in an individual manner suited to their style and their students' abilities. These appear to be very important reasons to think in terms of the three levels of generality for suggesting goals for the bigger overall program, instructional units, and specific activities. Within the three levels of goal statement there are other models and ideas which can assist the adult curriculum worker. The first level to be discussed is the general level.

General Level. As suggested above, the general level sets the stage for program development for a longer period of time. This general, abstract level is also the place where some consensus can and should be reached regarding what is of value to adult students

in a certain program effort and what should be taught/
learned in the curriculum. It is like an umbrella over
an entire program because it serves as an overriding
reference system for what should take place in that
program or in some cases school or center. Adult educators in their everyday instructional activities can
refer from time to time to the general level goals to
see if what they are doing is contributing to them.
This then represents a more complete effort on the part
of adult educators to meet significant goals in a more
coherent manner, and does in fact contribute to the
accountability process for entire adult education programs. Finally, it serves as a good transition level
from the philosophical expressions derived in the
rationale to the actual precision learning experiences
at the intermediate level. These are values which are
important to actual curriculum building, and it brings
more precision and awareness to the process.

General level goals can be stated in a variety of
ways after consensus by all decision makers has been
reached. They need not have the precision of behavioral
objectives, but they should be clear enough to give
direction to other levels of goal stating and in turn
instruction. Keeping them general and abstract not only
assists in gaining agreement as to their value, but
gives adult education curriculum builders the freedom
to develop individual goals and strategies for their
attainment.

Little has been done regarding a model for general
level goals for education of all adults. However, a
modification of the eighteen general goals developed
by the Phi Delta Kappa[4] might elicit some thinking on
the part of adult education curriculum builders. Some

examples of general goals for adult education programs and schools are suggested below which may serve as springboards for a statement of general goals for a given institution.

This adult education program (or center) in working with adult clients will:

1. Develop an awareness of civic rights and responsibilities and of the duties of a good citizen.

2. Develop an awareness of and the ability to adjust to the changing demands of society.

3. Develop skills in reading, writing, speaking and listening.

4. Develop the abilities to examine and use information and to think, reason, and solve pertinent problems.

5. Develop understanding and skills in family responsibilities and living.

6. Develop appreciation and respect for the worth and dignity of those individuals with whom we work and live.

7. Develop skills to enter a specific field of work, and provide an awareness of opportunities and requirements related to a specific field.

8. Develop the understanding and skills of being a good manager of money, property, and resources.

9. Develop a desire for learning now and in the future and of becoming a continuous, independent learner.

10. Develop the ability and skills to use leisure time productively.

11. Develop an understanding of good health and safety practices for oneself and one's family.

12. Develop the abilities for cultural appreciation of the arts and effective expression of ideas and the arts.

13. Develop the abilities to gain information needed for making job selections and for using the information and available counseling services related to the selection of a job.

14. Develop self-understanding, self-respect, and positive standards of personal character.

15. Develop a background and skills in the use of numbers, natural sciences, mathematics, and the social sciences for personal use and advancement.

16. Develop the skills for continuous employment in a given field or fields and for updating the required skills in a consistent manner.

The above sixteen general goals are only examples of what an adult education institution might define to guide programs or larger segments of instruction for adult clients who participate in the learning experiences. A careful review of these goals by practicing educators of adults might lead to some concern because they probably are different than usually specified. For one thing they are much broader than just getting an adult to pass a GED test, or teaching a person how to weld, or even teaching people of foreign origin to communicate in basic English. They are more comprehensive. Secondly, they are subject matter free in most cases. They set overall directions regardless of the substantive matter to be taught.

They focus more on total outcomes for adults, including concern for behaviors in the cognitive, affective, and pyschomotor domains. They cover general functional areas of adult behavior. And, since the education of adults in various programs and institutions is rapidly emerging as a significant field of endeavor and one where more critical thought and constructive curriculum activity are required, it might be necessary to think about total outcomes, in terms of behaviors, for adult clients. With goals like these a more comprehensive set of learning experiences can be built to help the total adult. Obviously, not all sixteen will be defined to guide a single adult program or center. For example, several of the above goals could be stated for a GED preparatory program, a vocational program, or an enrichment program. With several goals guiding an entire program more behaviors may be developed on the part of the adult clients which could lead to more successful living in our democratic society. This is something to which educators of all adults should give serious consideration.

To gain the appropriate consensus for goals for an entire program effort, adult curriculum workers may use the above sixteen-goal statement model (with any additions deemed necessary) in some sort of instrument to ascertain the value expressions of all of the people involved, or they may simply request a priority rating from one through sixteen. In any event some meaningful and significant information should and can be derived regarding the wishes of what general goals should be placed in an adult institution's curriculum for achieving. Adult curriculum workers may also want to restate some of the general goal statements in better terms so

that the goals may be a little more explicit and clearer
in order to provide directions for the longer periods
of instruction for a program. This can be done without
losing the general meaning and thus provides flexibility
for individual curriculum building efforts. Once some
clear statements are defined and agreed upon to guide
the instructional program at the general level, a move
then in terms of statements for more precise objectives
to guide classroom instruction is required. This can
begin at the intermediate level.

Intermediate Level. Again, the intermediate level of goal
statement is designed to guide the teaching/learning
efforts for more precise, manageable packages of instruction. This is where goals are defined for the
development of behaviors in the cognitive, affective,
and psychomotor domains in some content or substantive
area of study. This is also the level where adult curriculum workers must translate general, overarching,
abstract goal expressions into more precise statements
of goals which can be achieved by adult students in
their educative process. The main concern here is that
the appropriate behaviors be defined in a content or
subject matter area which can accomplish the general
behaviors and which can provide the direction for
learning experiences for adult clients in a unit, module, semester, quarter, or perhaps a year of study.
Since goals set the stage for all other curriculum
development activities, carefully defining objectives
at this level is critical. These objectives will then
be central to the development of the learning packages
(units, modules, and so forth) and will be tied in with
content organization in a later chapter.

Since this level of goal statement is critical to the development of learning packages with which adult students interact, and since a measure of precision is needed to specify carefully this all-important phase of curriculum building, some systems to guide this activity are required. Some taxonomic systems in the affective, cognitive, and psychomotor domains do exist which appear to have the required precision to assist adult curriculum workers in this phase of their work.

In the taxonomies, which classify cognitive processes (thinking and mental processes), affective behavior (attitudinal aspects), and psychomotor processes (physical or motor skills), a hierarchical order exists whereby each category is included within the next higher categories. Further, these systems look at the processes and internalization factors and not at subject matter or the content variable. In other words, these three systems are actually free of subject matter in that they can be applied to any subject matter area. Their strength lies in the fact that they combine the logical, psychological, and educational factors in the case of the cognitive domain, the attitudinal and internal factors for the affective domain, and the perceptual and motor skills in the case of the psychomotor domain, into a total system for analysis and analytic goal statement. Further, comparisons and the interchange of curriculum experiences can be made when standard systems like these are utilized.

Goals in the Cognitive Domain. The cognitive domain is generally viewed as a category labeled "knowledge" and five categories of the skills and abilities to use this knowledge. An outline of the major components of the cognitive domain is as follows:

1.00 Knowledge

    1.10 Knowledge of Specifics

        1.11 Knowledge of Terminology
        1.12 Knowledge of Specific Facts

    1.20 Knowledge of Ways and Means of Dealing With Specifics

        1.21 Knowledge of Conventions
        1.22 Knowledge of Trends and Sequences
        1.23 Knowledge of Classifications and Categories
        1.24 Knowledge of Criteria
        1.25 Knowledge of Methodology

    1.30 Knowledge of the Universals and Abstractions in a Field

        1.31 Knowledge of Principles and Generalizations
        1.32 Knowledge of Theories and Structures

2.00 Comprehension

    2.10 Translation
    2.20 Interpretation
    2.30 Extrapolation

3.00 Application

4.00 Analysis

    4.10 Analysis of Elements
    4.20 Analysis of Relationships
    4.30 Analysis of Organizational Principles

5.00 Synthesis

    5.10 Production of a Unique Communication
    5.20 Production of a Plan, or Proposed Set of Operations
    5.30 Derivation of a Set of Abstract Relations

6.00 Evaluation

    6.10 Judgments in Terms of Internal Evidence
    6.20 Judgments in Terms of External Criteria[5]

    The above outline indicates that the first level
of cognition (Knowledge) deals with the knowing of bits
of information from rather simple facts to complex
theories. The second (Comprehension) indicates that
the knowledge defined at the first level is understood
by the learner and that this understanding can be
reflected in various cognitive tasks. Once something
is known and understood by the learner, it can be put
to use. Level three (Application) is actually taking
the understood information and applying it to other
new situations. Analysis occurs when applied information is broken down into component parts through
comparing, contrasting, or distinguishing and viewing
the information itself. Synthesis is actually the
mental transformation of information into some new or
different structure, design, pattern, or solution.
Finally, Evaluation is the making of judgments or
assessments on information based on some criteria
specified beforehand. The hierarchy thus exists and
moves from simply knowing something to making precise
personal judgments about information confronting the
adult learner.

    Since the hierarchy does exist, an adult learner
cannot apply or analyze anything until the knowledge
and comprehension of the subject are assured. The same
holds true for all categories within the cognitive
domain. Thus each category or level of cognition is
dependent on one(s) lower than it. This is important
to understand if adult educators wish to incorporate

higher cognitive tasks in the learning experiences of their students. Adult students must have experiences to gain lower cognitive information before utilizing such information at higher levels. Also, many adult learners will not move to higher thought processes without direct, planned experiences to get them to that level. This is part of the decision-making process in developing curriculum experiences for adult clients.

Adult curriculum workers must decide what levels of cognitive development will be necessary for an adult learner to acquire in a given unit of study. If just the knowing and understanding of the information in an area of study are sufficient, then goals or objectives can be stated which will direct the adult learner to move to these levels. However, if in another given area of study it appears necessary for adult students to produce something new or different, or if some careful decisions and judgments are required, then the students must have objectives stated for them to move them to that level. A knowledge of the cognitive behaviors required for adults to operate in a given subject or content area is very important for adult education curriculum workers at this point.

To bring some effective utilization to Bloom's taxonomy, adult curriculum workers need some guides or instrumentation for writing objectives for the intermediate level in the curriculum. Once the value decisions have been made regarding what kinds of thinking should take place within a course, unit, or module of study in a given subject area, these decisions should be translated into statements of objectives to be achieved by adult clients in a given program. Metfessel,

Michael, and Kirsner[6] have designed some needed instrumentation to facilitate the formulation of objectives within the framework of the cognitive domain which can be of great help to adult education curriculum workers.

These authors have identified appropriate action infinitives which correspond to the taxonomic classification identified by both the code number and terminology of the taxonomy, and then have offered some direct objects which can be expanded upon to cover the subject matter properly. The action infinitives actually set the cognitive tone or level desired and the direct objects assist in the treatment of the subject matter under study. For example, under the general level of Knowledge, infinitives and direct objects might appear thus:

Infinitives	Direct Objects
to acquire	vocabulary
to recall	examples
to recognize	causes
to identify	theories

The infinitives indicate that the student will "know" the information when instruction is completed and the direct objects cover the different levels within the major category.

For the Comprehension level some examples are:

Infinitives	Direct Objects
to give in own words	meanings
to restate	methods
to explain	representations
to rearrange	effects

Again, the infinitives in this category indicate that the adult students do in fact understand that which has been learned. Direct objects again give direction to the subject matter under study.

For the Application level:

Infinitives	Direct Objects
to apply	laws
to use	processes
to transfer	principles
to restructure	procedures

The infinitives suggest that the student will take the learned information (qualities of the direct object) and apply it to new situations.

For Analysis:

Infinitives	Direct Objects
to categorize	elements
to analyze	statements
to compare	relationships
to distinguish	arrangements

These infinitives move the adult learner to analyzing the given information which can be expanded with the help of the direct objects.

For Synthesis:

Infinitives	Direct Objects
to produce	patterns
to originate	compositions
to design	schemes
to develop	specifics

The above infinitives upon completion of some study will lead the learner to synthesize or propose some new or different ideas as defined with the help of the direct objects.

For Evaluation:

Infinitives	Direct Objects
to judge	accuracies
to assess	precision
to appraise	generalizations
to argue	alternatives

These infinitives cause the adult learner to operate at the highest level of cognition when judgments on subject matter are required.

The above are just some examples of action infinitives and qualifying direct objects. Others may be developed and used by adult curriculum workers as long as they preserve the cognitive level that is desired and assist in determining the quality of the appropriate subject area content. And, infinitives may be used with a variety of direct objects assuming, of course, that they fit together and make sense.

To utilize these infinitives and direct objects for specifying goals at the intermediate level, the following format might be incorporated. Simply state, "As a result of the study of (unit of subject matter), the adult students will be able (infinitive) the (direct object) of (a selected part of the content)."

To illustrate, some examples of objectives (with infinitives and direct objects italicized) for the intermediate level in each of the six levels of cognition follow:

As a result of the study of the Constitution, the adult students will be able *to identify* an *example* of the three branches of government. (Knowledge)

As a result of the study of the United States government, the adult students will be able *to explain* the *methods* of getting a legislative bill through Congress. (Comprehension)

As a result of the study of beginning art for adults, the adult students will be able *to apply* the *principles* of color and design in a water color painting. (Application)

As a result of the study of small engines, the adult students will be able *to compare and contrast* the various *elements* of a two-cycle engine with those of a four-cycle engine. (Analysis)

As a result of the study of the short story, the adult students will be able *to originate* a *composition* utilizing the characteristics and qualities of a short story. (Synthesis)

As a result of the study of the newspaper (for basic reading skill development), the adult students will be able *to judge* the *accuracies* of a given article based on criteria specified by the teacher. (Evaluation)

Cognitive goals can be stated in any area of study and again provide the direction for the development of mental processes in an instructional setting. When the development is complete the adult students will actually possess a "cognitive state." That is, the adult learners literally have the knowledge and the ability to use it stored away in their heads. To check to see if the cognitive state is present, some overt act will be necessary to display the behavior. In other words, the adult's mastery of a cognitive behavior will not be apparent until some overt act is performed, such as talking about it, writing about it on a piece of paper, or perhaps using it in some problem-solving situation.

At this point it should be obvious that a number of cognitive goals can be stated for a unit, semester,

or year of study in a given field of study. This will
be discussed in a later chapter when organizing content
is presented.

Goals in the Affective Domain. The affective domain deals
primarily with the change or inner growth of an adult
learner as the adult receives, becomes aware of, and
begins to adopt certain attitudes and principles which
in turn form selected value judgments. These value
judgments begin to affect the individual's behavior
because the adult will behave according to the value
system that he/she possesses. Upon the complete internalization of the value system the adult will be
characterized by a consistent behavior pattern or way
of life. All stimuli or ideas that confront the adult
learner will have some affect on the adult's behavior
depending on how the ideas are treated and if they fit
into the individual's value system. The affective domain is thus very important in the instructional process
because of its meaning for attitude formation and its
total affect on behavior patterns.

An outline of the major components of the domain
is as follows:

1.00 Receiving (Attending)

    1.10 Awareness
    1.20 Willingness to Receive
    1.30 Controlled or Selected Attention

2.00 Responding

    2.10 Acquiescence in Responding
    2.20 Willingness to Respond
    2.30 Satisfaction in Response

3.00 Valuing

> 3.10 Acceptance of a Value
> 3.20 Preference for a Value
> 3.30 Commitment (conviction)

4.00 Organization

> 4.10 Conceptualization
> 4.20 Organization of a Value System

5.00 Characterization by a Value or Value Complex

> 5.10 Generalized Set
> 5.20 Characterization[7]

In reviewing the above outline on the affective domain, it will be noted that the formation of attitudes and ultimately total behavioral characterization begins when an individual receives some external stimuli regarding some phenomenon into the personal perceptual screen. First an awareness of the stimuli is present. If the stimuli have some personal meaning, the individual will foster a willingness to receive them. If continued meaning is present the individual will afford selected attention to the stimuli. The next move from receiving is to responding if the phenomenon under consideration continues to affect the individual. First, the individual will perhaps give in (acquiesce) in the form of a response, but if continued meaning is present, the individual will express a willingness to respond and then a satisfaction in response to the phenomenon will follow.

At this point in the affective hierarchy, if the object or event (phenomenon) which the individual is perceiving takes on more personal meaning and gains in importance internally, the individual may begin to "value" it to some degree. Within the value category,

the first step for the individual would be accepting
the object or event; then a preference for the particular thing would be established. Finally, a commitment
to the phenomenon under investigation would be established internally by the individual. It would be important to a person being confronted with it.

Numerous objects and events confront people to
which a value is placed. Many times these values are
viewed as very important. Some values are more important than others and thus some conceptualizing and
organizing of values into a value system is necessary
and will occur. The value system develops as one
reviews what is important to the maintenance and en-
hancement of the self, and overt behavior will reflect
some of the more important values held by the individual. The overt behavior is seen as the characterization of the individual, or the way he/she appears
to operate consistently in many different situations.
The total characterization of the individual really is
the consistent overt behavioral (affective) state which
governs the individual's responses to a variety of
situations in a generally consistent and coherent
manner. This personal position is the highest order
of affective behavior.

The implications and perhaps complications of this
affective domain are many and varied for educators of
adults to consider. As one reviews the outline and
discussion presented above, it should be obvious that
it will be no easy task to move individual adult
learners during the instructional process to new attitudes and values in selected areas of study. Adults
will truly have to see the personal meaning of learning

something before a movement up the hierarchy is possible. Adult learners have had considerable time to formulate their own values and value systems, and to introduce new information into the affective realm and expect some change in the behavior will not be easy. Adult educators themselves can review their own personal feelings, attitudes, and values and reflect upon what it would take to foster change in them. Although difficult to do, a readiness on the parts of adult learners and careful curriculum programming by adult educators can bring about change in this important domain of behavior.

Another complicating factor is that it will take time to change behaviors in this domain. Attitude change and the development of new values do not just happen overnight, particularly in an instructional setting. Adult clients must have time to review their existing beliefs and look carefully at new ideas before they will incorporate them into their current system of values. Whereas new cognitive and psychomotor behaviors can be developed rather quickly, it will take time for adult clients, particularly, to experience change and growth in affective behaviors. This has real meaning for short-term learning experiences for adults where higher order affective behaviors are deemed necessary. In some cases, there just might not be enough time to assimilate new affective behaviors; adult students may not have sufficient time or experiences to reexamine information and thus develop new values and place them into their system of operating under short-term course experience situations. Precise goal stating in this domain is required first on the

part of adult education curriculum workers, and then
the delivery system (instructional package) can be
defined.

Adult curriculum builders will have to assess carefully the quality of affective behavior which appears
to be necessary in a given subject area and then establish the goal level. As in all domains moving the
adult client to the utmost level in a given area may
not be necessary. And in some cases it might be very
important to have the adult learner operate at a high
level in order to function properly or adequately in
society as a result of formal study in a given area of
adult study. Critical analysis and decision making are
required in this area of adult curriculum development
activity. Again, it should be kept in mind that the
goals give the direction to the instructional process.

The measurement of the affective goals, which will
be discussed later, is also not an easy task. If adult
students are aware that certain affective growth is
required to complete a given course of study, then the
student might "fake" the required behavior in order to
"pass" the course or program. Care must be taken in not
only teaching toward a certain affective level, but
also in attempting to gather evidence to see if the
behavior did in fact result from the formal instruction.

Even though difficulties arise in using the affective domain and taxonomy in adult education curriculum
building, it is still very important to think about
and incorporate into all experiences. Beside its
effect on attitude formation, it is also important in
that all learners respond to some degree to what they
are being exposed to. Stimuli are ever-present in a

learning experience and students will react to them in some fashion. They may be "turned on" or "turned off" by the learning experience confronting them; they are in fact making judgments regarding the value or lack of value of what they are perceiving mentally in a formal instructional situation. Just as the readers of this book are making judgments about the value or lack of value for its use in curriculum development work in adult education, adult students will also offer mental judgments regarding the value of their instructional content whether they are required or not. When adult students are put through some cognitive or psychomotor learning experience they are judging the value of it, and judging it in their minds. So beside going through the mental processes associated with cognitive and psychomotor experiences they are also going through mental processes that help to establish the value of the experiences. This close interrelationship of the behavioral domains is very important to consider, and since the affective stimuli are ever-present in all learning situations, curriculum workers must be aware of this and direct the stimuli toward positive directions in terms of growth for their adult clients.

A final point on the development of affective behaviors is that the result is again a "state," an affective state. The affective state is housed within the mind (not the heart) of the adult client after the instruction has occurred. Adult educators will not be aware of the new affective behavior until some overt behavior is displayed by the adult. Educators do not know if students are receiving, responding, or valuing

something until the student performs some overt act to
indicate at what point the affective behavior rests.

As in the cognitive domain, some instrumentation
will be required to assist adult curriculum workers
to bring some precision to the utilization of the
affective taxonomy in goal stating at the intermediate
level. This instrumentation is present and can set
some guides for the effective development of goals for
instructional units and modules or semester or year-
long packages of instruction for adult clients. Again,
once some decisions have been made regarding what level
of affective behavior seems appropriate for a selected
area of study to achieve, a move to specify certain
affective behaviors is required.

Metfessel, Michael, and Kirsner[8] have again identified certain action infinitives which correspond to the
taxonomic classification identified by both the code
number and terminology of the taxonomy, and then offered
some direct objects which can be expanded upon to cover
the subject matter properly.

Within the first level of Receiving some examples
might be:

Infinitives	Direct Objects
to differentiate	sounds
to accumulate	models
to accept	examples
to listen (for)	alternatives

The infinitives indicate that after instruction the
students will have received and have given some attention to the stimuli associated with the subject matter
that was presented. The direct objects help to give

some guidance as to the way the subject matter will be emphasized.

Within the Responding category some examples are:

Infinitives	Direct Objects
to comply (with)	directions
to volunteer	presentations
to practice	games
to spend leisure time in	instruments

The infinitives at this level indicate that some response is being made to the objects and events under study, and the direct objects again offer some help to the subject matter.

Within the Valuing category some examples are:

Infinitives	Direct Objects
to increase measured proficiency in	artistic productions
to assist	projects
to support	viewpoints
to argue	irrelevancies

These infinitives indicate that some value is seen in the subject under study after it has been completed, with direct objects giving direction to subject matter areas where some value may be attached.

At the Organization level some examples are:

Infinitives	Direct Objects
to compare	standards
to balance	goals
to organize	systems
to formulate	approaches

The key words at this level indicate that some organization is given to various values being emphasized by some formal learning experiences.

Finally, at the Characterization level some examples are:

Infinitives	Direct Objects
to change	plans
to be rated high by peers in	integrity
to avoid	excesses
to resolve	conflicts

The important key words at this level reflect that adult learners will be characterized by certain behaviors which will demonstrate that they feel and believe and are ready to support (or not support) overtly some significant object or event in their environment. These words suggest that the ultimate affective behavior will be displayed in a selected area of living.

The above are some examples of key words that can be used to assist with goal specification in the affective domain. Others can be designed for use as long as they are geared to the appropriate level desired by curriculum workers.

The same basic format for specifying goals in the affective domain at the intermediate level can be used as was suggested for the cognitive area. Some freedom might be taken with the infinitives, verbs, and nouns to make the goals much smoother statements of outcomes. Some examples of affective goal statements at the five different levels are as follows:

As a result of the study of the United States

Constitution, the adult students will be able *to differentiate* three *examples* of the importance of the Bill of Rights. (Receiving)

As a result of a piano class for adults, the adult students will be willing *to practice* their *pianos (instruments)* for a half hour or more every day. (Responding)

As a result of a class on stock market investments, the adult students will be able *to argue* all of the *viewpoints* about careful financial planning before moving into substantial stock market investments. (Valuing)

As a result of a vocational-technical program, the adult students will be able *to organize* their *goals* for the world of work and proceed according to this organization. (Organization)

As a result of a business management program, the adult students will *be rated high by peers* in their field on *integrity* in business practices. (Characterization)

Goals in the Psychomotor Domain. Numerous goals in adult education programs suggest that the performance of motor or physical skills will be the outcome of instruction. These skills are found in vocational-technical areas, aesthetic areas, recreational and leisure areas, as well as others. These skills are important to adults as they function in everyday living, be it on or off the job, in the home or outside the home, and in serious and not so serious activities. Because of their importance, they should receive careful attention in adult education curriculum development work and not be left to chance. A taxonomic system has been devised to assist adult education curriculum workers in bringing more awareness and precision to their curriculum work. An

outline of the major components of the psychomotor domain which can be used at the intermediate level of goal
statement is as follows:

1.00 Perception

    1.10 Sensory Stimulation

        1.11 Auditory
        1.12 Visual
        1.13 Tactile
        1.14 Taste
        1.15 Smell
        1.16 Kinesthetic

    1.20 Cue Selection
    1.30 Translation

2.00 Set

    2.10 Mental
    2.20 Physical Set
    2.30 Emotional Set

3.00 Guided Response

    3.10 Imitation
    3.20 Trial and Error

4.00 Mechanism

5.00 Complex Overt Response

    5.10 Resolution of Uncertainty
    5.20 Automatic Performance

6.00 Adaptation

7.00 Origination[9]

    The above outline suggests that the development of
psychomotor behaviors begins with the simple perception
or becoming aware of objects, qualities, and relations
through the sense organs. This is basic to motor activity. After the senses have been stimulated by the

objects in one's environment, a decision is made as to
what cues one must respond to in order to satisfy the
requirements of the task at hand. After the cues have
been selected the mental processes of determining the
meaning of the cues received for action follow. After
the perceiving process is complete, the adult learner
will move to a set of readiness for a particular kind
of action or experience. This includes a mental set or
readiness to perform an act, a physical readiness in
terms of making anatomical adjustments, and an emotional
set or readiness in terms of a favorable attitude to the
motor acts taking place.

The guided response category is the one where an individual either under the guidance of an instructor or
based on a model or some criteria makes an overt behavioral act. This could occur through imitation with the
execution of an act coming after the performance by another person of the act, or by trial and error. Trial
and error usually comes with some rationale for each response in the act until an appropriate response is
achieved.

Mechanism is when a learned response has become habitual. At this point the adult learner has achieved a
degree of confidence and proficiency in the performance
of the act. The act then becomes part of a repertoire
of possible responses to stimuli and the demands of various situations where the response is an appropriate one.

When the psychomotor behavior becomes more sophisticated, the complex overt response comes into play.
This is when the adult learner can perform a motor act
that is considered complex because of the movement
pattern required. A high degree of skill has been at-
tained at this point. The resolution of uncertainty

comes when the act is performed without hesitation of the adult learner to get a mental picture of the task sequence. Automatic performance is when the adult learner performs a finely coordinated motor skill with a great deal of muscle control and ease.

The adaptation level arrives when the adult learner alters personal motor activities to meet the demands of new problem situations requiring a physical or motor skill. Finally, the ultimate psychomotor behavior, origination, is when the adult can create new motor acts or ways of manipulating materials out of the abilities, understandings, and skills developed in the psychomotor area.

Again, a hierarchy is present in this taxonomic classification which must be observed in the specification of goals and in the programming of learning experiences. Treatment must be afforded to lower level psychomotor goals before an adult learner can operate at a higher level such as adaptation or origination. The careful movement of adult students up the psychomotor ladder is required before they can function adequately in any given content area.

Decisions as to what level the adult learner should acquire in the psychomotor domain after formal instruction in any given area of study again rest with curriculum workers after a thorough assessment is made. Once the level of behavior is determined, goal specification can begin.

Some basic instrumentation is available which can assist adult curriculum workers in specifying goals or objectives in the psychomotor domain at the intermediate level. This instrumentation[10] again identifies action infinitives which correspond to the taxonomic classification and then offers some direct objects to cover the subject matter properly. The infinitives set the tone or level of desired behavior and the direct objects aid in the treatment of the subject area under consideration. Application should take place in any subject area associated with psychomotor behaviors. The following illustrations should assist adult curriculum workers in their curriculum-building efforts.

For the general level of Perception some examples of key words are as follows:

Infinitives	Direct Objects
to recognize	parts
to detect	differences
to identify	relationships
to become aware of	shapes

With these infinitives the focus is placed on the initial perceiving or becoming aware of objects, qualities, and relations as a result of instruction. The direct objects assist with the more precise definition of the objects, qualities, or relations under consideration.

For the level called Set, some examples are:

Infinitives	Direct Objects
to focus	movements
to locate	positions
to set up	tools
to select	directions

These infinitives offer guidance to goal stating at this level in the fact that they suggest a preparatory adjustment or readiness for a particular kind of learning experience. The direct objects help to qualify the subject matter involved at this level.

For the Guided Response level of psychomotor behavior the following key words are examples:

Infinitives	Direct Objects
to imitate	demonstrations
to reproduce	examples
to model	patterns
to approximate	movements

These infinitives set the tone whereby adult learners will be able to perform certain psychomotor acts under the guidance of an instructor or by trial and error when instruction is completed. The direct objects bring precision to the subject matter that is taught.

For the Mechanism level some examples follow:

Infinitives	Direct Objects
to assemble	parts
to set up	procedures
to manipulate	steps
to shape	materials

The infinitives at this mechanism level should indicate that a learned response is fairly well habitual in nature. The adult learner has proficiency and confidence as a result of instruction. The direct objects aid in determining the level of behavior as it relates to subject matter.

For the Complex Overt Response category examples are:

Infinitives	Direct Objects
to coordinate	operations
to adjust	equipment
to regulate	operations
to combine	multiple adjustments

These infinitives indicate that after instruction and experience the adult learner can perform complex motor acts. A high degree of skill is reflected in the infinitives. The direct objects also indicate more complex treatment of the subject matter.

At the Adaptation level some examples of key words are:

Infinitives	Direct Objects
to adapt	operations
to convert	procedures
to integrate	sequences
to standardize	steps

These infinitives indicate that the adult learner adapted to new situations by altering motor activities to meet new demands in problem situations. The direct objects suggest a broader use of the subject matter under study.

Finally, for the Origination level, the following key words are offered:

Infinitives	Direct Objects
to create	patterns
to design	movements
to invent	systems
to originate	procedures

These infinitives reflect that the highest order
of psychomotor behavior is achieved because new motor
acts or ways of manipulating materials have resulted.
The direct objects reflect the broad application of the
subject matter.

The above again are examples of key words which
can be used in varying combinations to specify goals
in the psychomotor domain at the intermediate level.
Other key words may be defined and used as long as they
preserve the level desired for the outcomes of instruction. To utilize these infinitives and direct objects
for goal stating, the same basic format as described
above may be used. Some examples of objectives for the
psychomotor domain specified at the seven different
levels are as follows:

As a result of a course in beginning painting,
adult students will be able *to identify* the *differences* in
the basic colors used in the field of art. (Perception)

As a result of a beginning course in auto mechanics,
adult students will be able *to set up* physically the
tools to gap spark plugs. (Set)

As a result of a course in the fundamentals of golf,
adult students will be able *to imitate* the basic *movements*
required in using woods on the tee and the fairway.
(Guided Response)

As a result of a course in upholstery, refinishing,
and restyling, adult students will be able *to manipulate*
easily the *materials* needed to upholster a leather
chair. (Mechanism)

As a result of an advanced aviation technology
course, adult students will be able *to coordinate* the
equipment needed for the maintenance of small aircraft.
(Complex Overt Response)

As a result of the terminal building technology
course, adult students will be able *to integrate* all
operations required for the construction of a new house
of any size. (Adaptation)

As a result of the advanced course in dressmaking, adult students will be able *to create new patterns* for clothing for formal use. (Origination)

The use of the psychomotor domain and in turn the accompanying taxonomic system has broad application for any and all adult learning curriculum building. Many psychomotor behaviors are striven for in this field of education because of their meaning for adults who are trying to function and compete successfully in society. It appears that numerous psychomotor behaviors are needed by adults for everyday living. With the use of a taxonomy, more precision can be brought to the specification of goals to govern the directions of a learning package for adults. Again, the decision must be made by adult education curriculum workers as to what level of psychomotor behavior is necessary for adult students to achieve within a given area of study. When this decision is made, adult curriculum builders can then move to more precise goal stating to give the direction for significant instruction.

A final concern again about this domain of behavior as with others is that instruction will lead to a psychomotor state. An adult may be able to gap correctly spark plugs based on some standardized specifications but the instructor will not know until the learner gives an overt demonstration of the learned behavior. However, the beauty of the psychomotor domain rests with the fact that this behavior category requires overt performance of a motor or physical skill. And, generally the learning of the skill requires overt action throughout the process. But at the higher order level of this area of behaviors, it is possible to possess the "knowledge" at the adaptation or origination level without "putting it into action." As might be expected the measurement of learned behavior in this domain is much easier too because of its being of a physical or motor nature.

These three taxonomic systems appear to have great meaning for guiding the statement of goals at the course development level. They can provide significant direction for the various packages of instruction that are given to adults in all learning situations. Since goals or objectives should dictate the direction of a learning experience for adults, precise instruments like these can significantly contribute to more precise course development work.

Further, these taxonomies serve as excellent referents for goals at the specific level and for everyday instruction. In fact, some of the intermediate goals could actually be part of the specific level goals when a course or module of study is trying to build higher order behaviors. Because of the hierarchical nature of the domains, lower order behaviors are required before moving to a higher level. The lower order objectives will thus probably serve as guides to the daily instructional activities.

Assessment of the growth of adult students as a result of instruction can be greatly enhanced at the end of a course or module of study when more carefully defined objectives are specified in the beginning. Although these taxonomies may lack the real precision of behavioral objectives, they can make quite explicit the general behaviors that should result at the end of a course experience. This definitely makes the adult curriculum worker's task much easier to perform.

As will be noted later the objectives for a single course will probably incorporate statements from all three domains. Numerous courses in the vocational-technical-occupational, general, and adult basic areas require that behaviors are formed in all three domains. The specification of all appropriate objectives for a course of study will reflect this and lead to a more complete learning experience for adult students. The complete development of a course utilizing these taxonomies can lead to considerable interchange between adult programs and centers and educators because a single and common "language" is utilized. This can add immeasurably to the adult and continuing education profession.

Upon careful thinking about and development of goals at the intermediate level, the next step is goal specification at the specific, short-term, day-to-day level. These goals provide the transition from "paper" planning to actual classroom instruction. Some attention is devoted to specific goals in the following section which will tie in with the following chapter on instruction and content organization.

Specific Level. One of the strengths of the three-level model of generality for specifying goals is that there is considerable freedom present at the specific level for individual teachers and their direct work with adult students. The teachers can define goals or objectives at this level based on their own unique abilities and strengths and the needs and entering behavior of their students. They can analyze the needs and exercise options for their students' direct learning experiences, and at the same time they have an overriding set of goals at the intermediate level which gives them the general direction for the learning experiences. In other words, there are and probably have to be a number of different approaches to teaching a concept to individual students in an adult class, and this can best be accomplished when adult teachers after a careful analysis of all factors proceed to define the objectives and strategies for the development of the new behavior. Thus, according to this model many of the specific objectives will probably be developed by the teachers in their day-to-day activities. This, however, does not preclude the development and specification of specific objectives by a group of teachers (curriculum workers) when some commonality is desired for a certain course or subject where multiple sections are present, or when certain courses or subjects are in sequential order and a series of objectives are required or seen as very important for adults to acquire. In the latter case the modification and individualization would come as an individual teacher begins work with a certain set of adult clients in a classroom setting. In any case some ideas and guides for goal specification at this level will help adult educators in their direct teaching activities.

Perhaps the biggest concern for adult curriculum workers is in regard to the level of precision and specificity desired and/or required for objectives for classroom instruction. More precise statements to govern this level might encourage the use of behavioral objectives in guiding daily learning experiences. And, since the basic job of educators is to help people to learn, or change to new behavior, the use of objectives stated in terms of terminal behaviors might be the best avenue to follow. Behavioral objectives state what kind of behavior will result after the instruction has taken place, and are used so that observable adult behavior is in measurable terms. They also give a specific direction for the adult teacher and the adult student before actual instruction begins.

A format with certain steps is available for adult curriculum workers to use in the development of behavioral objectives to be incorporated at the specific level.[11] These authors suggest that "at the course level of instruction, the content needs to be operationalized. This requires (1) writing behavioral objectives stating content in sentence form to relate what the adult student is to do, and (2) wording the objectives in such a fashion that the adult student must do something which is observable."[12] The six steps identified in this process are discussed below.

Step 1. Use the adult student as the subject of behavioral objectives. The objective should communicate specifically what the adult is expected to do as a result of the learning. Further, objectives written with the adult in mind help to identify appropriate learning activities. Last the objective describes a change in behavior, and the subject of that behavior change is the adult. In focusing on the adult student, the sought behavior change is consistent with the clientele for whom the objective is intended.

Step 2. Identify and state observable responses expected of the adult student. A behavioral objective describes the task, knowledge, or attitude for which the adult is being trained. For this reason, most behavioral objectives are written in action or doing form. Action verbs are used to help convey activity and accomplishment on the part of the adult.[13]

The first two steps focus curriculum workers' attention on the fact that the adult student, rightfully so, is the key person in the learning situation, and that observable responses are important to see if learning has taken place on the part of the adult client. Action verbs should be precise and convey a specific effort on the part of the adult learner. These two steps taken together would result in a partial statement or the beginning of a stated behavior objective such as: a) the adult student is able to calibrate . . .; b) the adult student is able to adjust . . .; c) the adult student is able to regulate. . . .

The next step will bring more precision to the objective by focusing on tasks and operations. It is:

Step 3. Identify and state tasks as operations to be performed. The objectives specify the learning components of a given task by stating the distinct capabilities or actions needed to perform the particular task. Further, it is important to identify for each capability a body of necessary knowledge, principles, and attitudes, relevant to its successful achievement. Welders, for example, need to know that lighting an arc is dependent not only upon the cylinders being readied, but also upon a desire and willingness to do a good job of welding.[14]

Adding the task or operation to the partial behavioral statement would indicate what the adult learner has to do in terms of performance. Some examples at this point would illustrate the partial statement thus: a) the adult student is able to recall the twenty-six letters of the English alphabet . . .; b) the adult student is able to adjust a table saw . . .; c) the adult student is able to translate these twenty-five words in Spanish into English. . . .

Step 4. Identify and state how behavior is to be demonstrated so that learning can be observed. The way in which learned behavior is to be exhibited may not always reflect the exact way the behavior will be used outside the educational setting, but it should approximate as closely as possible the setting eventually used for the performance.[15]

This step suggests that a qualifier be added to the partial behavioral statement to suggest how the behavior will actually be demonstrated to see if learning has taken place. Some key terms within this category which demonstrate how the behavior is to be demonstrated are as follows: a) by writing on paper; b) by matching; c) by performing.

The next step encourages the writer of objectives to identify the standards or quality of the outcome desired. This is as follows:

Step 5. Identify and state the standards or quality of outcome desired. The behavioral objective should identify the level that will be used to judge successful performance of the task. The standard of performance should be specific and observable, so that the adult student and teacher can recognize achievement.[16]

Such examples of standards are: a) within 10 percent accuracy; b) in accordance with specified hospital standards; and c) according to the adult teacher's specifications.

The final step for drafting behavioral statements to guide objectives at the specific level is:

Step 6. Write the behavioral objective in a complete sentence. Once the various components of behavioral objectives are identified, they need to be put together in sentence form. Beginning with a focus on the adult student, the behavioral objective needs to include the desired performance, an active description, the means by which the behavior is to be exhibited, and the criteria for measurement.[17]

In following these steps carefully some clearly stated behavioral statements will result which give direction to both the teacher and student, describe what the adult student needs to do, and indicate what the quality of the new behavior should be. Very explicit statements help immeasurably when the instructional process begins, and further aid in the measurement or evaluation process too. Some examples of completed statements are: a) the adult student is able to translate these twenty-five words in Spanish into English on paper with 100 percent accuracy; b) the adult student is able to identify the four types of concrete blocks by pointing to the appropriate blocks when each type is named and do this without error; c) the adult student is able to draw out with a syringe 1 cc., 1 1/2 cc., and 2 cc. of liquid from a vial with 100 percent accuracy.

Although behavioral objectives appear to have considerable merit for giving direction to the teaching/learning process, they could be detrimental to the total process if certain cautions are not exercised by adult educators. Dumas[18] in supporting the use of these kinds of objectives offers some cautions and concerns worthy of the attention of adult curriculum workers. Some of his concerns relevant to adult education are discussed below.

Many times a behavioral objective is judged by its measurability; that is, if it is not easily measured, then it cannot be taught or is not worth teaching. Using measurability as a criterion of worth or value is incorrect in that other criteria should be employed to judge the validity of an objective. Even though some valid objectives may be difficult to measure (that is, affective statements) they still should be taught and measured as best as can be done.

Also, behavioral objectives at times are stated so
narrowly that trivial information at the knowledge level
is derived, and the broad conceptual outcomes are
missing. This implies that less learning or less complex
learning is desired. Adult education curriculum workers
must be aware of this when thinking about and defining
these objectives. The use of the three taxonomies discussed above should insure that broader outcomes will
result. Further, behavioral objectives should be seen
as minimal statements of expectation, never as the outer
limits of learning. Adult students under the guidance
of their teachers should be encouraged to go beyond
simple learning and explore the implications, meaning,
and use of the conceptual information. This can be
accomplished, however, in objectives stated by adult
curriculum workers in the very beginning. This is part
of the planning process. The aid given by the three-
level goal model too will help give broader emphasis to
the behavioral outcomes desired in adult clients.

The process of working with and defining objectives
at the specific level, like all other phases of curriculum development work, is very important and not an easy
task. But because of its critical nature care must be
taken in this process; it provides the very important
direction for the direct learning experiences given to
adults. And, again it provides for the transition from
the planning stage to the actual activity in a classroom.

Summary. Considerable attention has been given to the
process of defining and organizing adult education
curriculum and instructional goals in this chapter.

This is because the process is of critical concern to adult education curriculum builders and sets the stage for what follows. Various guides and models have been presented which should alert curriculum people to the need for defining goals at different levels and in different domains. A potentially significant and useful model was developed which is summarized below:

Goals
General level   Goals in the cognitive domain
Intermediate level   Goals in the affective domain
Specific level   Goals in the psychomotor domain

FIGURE 4.1 *Goal Statements for Adult Education*

Again, the above discussion gives direction to thinking about and organizing goals, but not any suggestions as to what the goals at any level should be. This process must come from the adult education curriculum workers and others after careful study. Once goals have been defined and organized the next process in curriculum building is developing the delivery system or ways to accomplish the goals. This system, instruction and content organization, is the focus of the following chapter.

5 / Instruction and Content Organization

This chapter will focus attention on two major segments of the general curriculum model, that of the instructional act and that of the organization of the
content for more effective teaching and learning. These
segments comprise a major element of the curriculum
structure and deserve very careful attention as this
element gets to the heart of program development and
the delivery of learning experiences to adult students.

INSTRUCTION

As suggested above, adult instruction is the delivery
system for the curriculum, program, or learning unit of
study. Although it may not be perceived as actual curriculum building, there are a variety of factors involved which are important for curriculum workers as
they design experiences for adult students. And, to have
a totally successful curriculum design, the instructional system must be carefully organized and presented
to adult students. Therefore, some discussion will be
presented on organizing and planning instruction for
effective utilization in the adult learning situation.

Overview of Instructional Model. Again to lend some precision to the education of all adults some systematic framework for the instructional process should be defined to ensure that all variables are given attention and placed in a working model.

In brief the model (see Figure 5.1) begins in the planning stages with the assessment of the entering behavior of the adult student in conjunction with the statement of goals. These two operations should take place in conjunction with one another so that the adult client can have goals, however defined, which are attainable according to his/her previous learning and experience. If adult teachers do not look at the entering behavior, their goals may be too difficult to attain on the parts of their students and thus the instruction will fall short. At the other extreme, the goals may not present a challenge or the adult learner may already possess the expressed behaviors before instruction begins. Therefore, assessment and goal statement should be done together so as to define the best possible learning experience for the adult learner.

Once the entering behavior has been assessed and the goals have been clearly and concisely stated, the definition of appropriate learning experiences for achieving the goals is done. In defining the unit to be learned and the procedures, the necessary content and materials are selected, tasks and strategies are selected or invented, and all tasks and strategies to accomplish the goals are sequenced and ordered for effective learning by adult students.

When the learning unit and procedures are defined by the teacher or cooperatively with the adult students

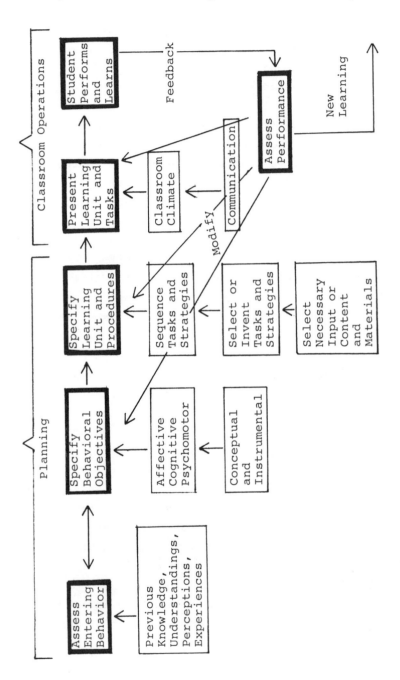

FIGURE 5.1 Adult Instructional *Model*[1]

the move is then made to presenting these to the students for accomplishment. This is the actual classroom or similar learning situation which involves the interaction of the adult teacher, the adult students and the content which is to be learned. Within the classroom learning situation a climate conducive to learing should be established and maintained which is appropriate for adult learners. Also, communication is involved and important to adult learning. The next step involves the adult student performing the various tasks and learning what has been defined in the goal statement. This performance could involve the pronouncing of some words in English in an English as a second language class, solving a problem in an accounting class, the building of something in a vocational-technical class, or simply acquiring for future use some knowledge in a real estate class. In any case the student must have the opportunity to perform the task previously defined. Then some provision should be made to determine to what degree the adult students did what they set out to do. The final component is evaluation or assessment of performance. If the performance did not measure up to the stated objectives, then some modification is necessary in terms of the goals, the nature of the learning unit, or the presentation of the individual unit. Modification will be necessary to ensure that the adult students learned what was defined for them. If the adult students have performed at a designated level, then they are ready for new learning and the instructional model repeats itself. Actually the terminal behavior or performance of this learning unit could be the entering behavior of a new unit of learning.

The model itself actually argues for individualized instruction simply because adult students come to a learning situation with varied entering behavior and generally different goals for learning. With this in mind some discussion of the various components of the model will be discussed.

Assessing Entering Behavior and Specifying Instructional Objectives. As suggested above, these two processes should be carried out simultaneously so that the objectives are compatible with the entering behavior of the adult students. This permits more effective learning in that a realistic assessment of behavior will allow for goals that are within reach of the adults and not "below or above" their capabilities. Consonance should occur in these important processes so that all adults can achieve. This may not perhaps be considered a hard and fast rule because some sound and important objectives both to the adult student and the total learning unit may emerge which in the judgment of the adult teacher must be taught. In many of these cases if objectives are designated as important and the entering behavior is not present, some pre-instruction or review may be necessary to raise the entering behavior to become compatible with the objectives. Either avenue is sound as long as the entering behavior is such that meaningful instruction can occur to achieve the selected objectives. This is why the reversible arrow is present in the basic instructional model.

As suggested in chapter 4, it is important to think in terms of behavior when stating objectives for adult students. It is the teacher's job to help adults learn, and learning can be defined as that of changing behavior

to some desired end. This is consistent with a usable
definition of teaching by N. L. Gage. He defines teaching as "any interpersonal influence at changing the
ways in which other persons can or will behave."[2] Thus,
behavior becomes all-important as adult teachers begin
to think in terms of instructional process.

The entering behavior of the student or, as De Cecco
refers to it, the entering performances is the level of
knowledge, skill, and attitude that the adult student
brings to the new instruction. De Cecco states:

Entering behavior describes the behaviors the student
must have acquired before he can acquire particular
new terminal behaviors. More simply, entering behavior
describes the present status of the student's knowledge and skill in reference to a future status the
teacher wants him to attain. Entering behavior, therefore, is where the instruction must always begin.[3]

Observing and measuring the entering behavior or level
of performance are not often done by teachers and are
not easy tasks, but this process must be done because
the adult teacher's job is to move the student from
entering performance to that of the desired terminal
performance (the objective). As suggested earlier, the
entering performances for new instruction are the end
products of previous instruction so the adult teacher
should have an awareness of what the level of his/her
students' entering behavior is. However, listing the
needed performances for the new instruction makes explicit exactly what is requisite for instruction to
begin and brings considerable precision to the teaching
act. Thus, listing the behaviors is important and
De Cecco suggests further that "a list of entering behavior reveals two characteristics; the statements are
explicit and refer to specific, observable performances

and a list as a whole is generally more comprehensive than the corresponding list of terminal performances."[4] These two characteristics of observable performances and comprehensiveness are important for the adult teacher and adult curriculum worker to keep in mind because with a complete listing of entering performances the teacher's task of accomplishing the new performance is clearer and greatly enhanced. This, therefore, has very definite curriculum building implications, because as curriculum workers begin to think about and define objectives at this specific level they must also think about and define the required entering level performances.

There are other aspects of adult students and their behavior which obviously affect their classroom learning such as motivation, readiness, individual differences, cultural background, and experiences in life. These must be considered in each individual student. The teacher must give consideration to the total entering performances of an adult student and coordinate them with the appropriate terminal objectives of each learning unit. Upon the specification of objectives the attention must focus on the required entering performances and the assessment must seek to determine if the performances are present. If entering behavior is not sufficient, again the adult teacher can review with the student to recall previous knowledge, provide additional instruction to update the student, or reject or modify the stated objective. Only when these steps are taken can the adult teacher be sure that meaningful instruction will take place.

Instructional objectives, objectives at the specific level, set the stage and provide the direction for the

instructional process. They define the kinds of behaviors that adult students should display at the end
of a learning unit of instruction. However, before
clear specification of the objectives can be made some
consideration must be given to the content variable and
its relationship to the defined terminal behavior. The
interrelationship of the new behavior and the content
or substantive matter to be learned is important as
every teaching activity has some content which influences adult students through their interaction with it.

Instrumental and Conceptual Goals. It could be strongly argued that behavior changes as adult students have the
opportunity to interact with their environment and the
objects and events in it. In the case of formal adult
instruction in the classroom the teacher provides the
various environmental conditions, both real and simulated, with which the student interacts; therefore,
the environmental conditions should depend upon the
kind of behavior desired. Some terminal behaviors may
be viewed as rather simple while others may be very
complex.

In the first case of rather simple behaviors,
largely reflexive in form, actual instrumental behavior
can be developed through various forms of operant
conditioning. This major category of behaviors requires
little in the way of logical conceptual content so
operant conditioning will effect the desired terminal
behavior. An example of terminal behavior in this
category is the act of performing multiplication of
three-digit numbers. Proper grammatical expression in
everyday living, writing correctly grammatically and
legibly, and translating foreign words into English

are also terminal behaviors which require little logical interaction with environmental conditions and content in the formation of the behaviors. It should be noted by adult education curriculum workers that these behaviors are important in this instrumental category and should not be slighted or downgraded. However, designing learning units for their acquisition is different and requires other moves than that of using conceptual objectives. Besides these rather simple instrumental behavioral objectives which the adult teacher can accomplish through operant conditioning techniques, more complex behaviors exist which require much different strategies to accomplish these behaviors.

As mentioned above behavior changes and learning takes place as adults interact with their environment. They perceive the objects and events in their environment, form concepts about them, use the concepts for making decisions, and actually act on their decisions. This more complex behavior results then from specifying conceptual goals (content) and, in turn, the true interaction with a certain environment condition. The conceptual goals are important because an adult's environment is composed of objects (termed structural concepts) and events (process concepts). An adult in an adult learning program can learn about machines, the stock market, adjectives, plants, job opportunities, the United States government, and sewing, which are the objects and events in his/her world. Forming concepts about objects and events gives the student the raw material with which to think about, judge, and act upon in the real world. Therefore, careful attention should be afforded conceptual information in curriculum building and in instructional processes, since this deals basically with the content or substantive matter to be learned.

Woodruff defines a concept as:

> . . . a relatively complete and meaningful idea in the mind of a person. It is an understanding of something. It is his own subjective product of his way of making meaning of things he has seen or otherwise perceived in his experiences. At its most concrete level it is likely to be a mental image of some actual object or event the person has seen. At its most abstract and complex level it is a synthesis of a number of conclusions he has drawn about his experiences with particular things.[5]

He further defines a *process* concept thus: "A concept of a process, event or behavior and the consequences it produces when it occurs."[6] And he defines a *structural* concept: "A concept of an object, relationship or structure of some kind."[7]

Some examples of process concepts in their proper form are as follows:

When the surfaces of the parts of certain metals are heated and are allowed to flow together, the metallic parts will unite (welding concept).

If the United State Senate and House of Representatives pass a bill and the President signs it, it then becomes law (Constitutional concept).

When an adult teacher specifies the content to be taught in a classroom in terms of conceptual statements, the actual teaching task is made easier because the direction is much clearer (teaching concept).[8]

Some examples of structural concepts in their proper form are as follows:

A bill of sale is a formal instrument for the conveyance or transfer of title to various goods or properties (business concept).

The normal body temperature of a human being is approximately 98.6° F. (nursing concept).

An instructional model brings into consideration some thought about entering behavior, goal statements, the learning unit and procedures, the presentation of the learning unit, adult performance of tasks, and assessment of outcomes (teaching concept).[9]

There are many advantages to utilizing these conceptual goals or statements in the curriculum building and instructional processes. First, the conceptual goals--structure and process--can actually describe all of the objects and events in an adult learner's environment and therefore can cover the knowledge or content variable with precision. The resulting effect is that the conceptual information can be identified as curriculum workers define a broad body of knowledge that an adult student should learn in a given subject area. These conceptual statements can be identified, tied together with the required terminal goal statements, and then brought into some logical order for teaching and learning in the curriculum building process. The instructional process then addresses its attention to each conceptual statement and resulting behavior and designs strategies for the learning of this new behavior. In other words curriculum workers can identify the appropriate content for a given area of study, place it into conceptual statements, state it in behavioral terms, bring some logical order to these statements, and have them ready for direct learning by adult students. Identifying and ordering these conceptual statements also helps in the entering-behavior assessment process. The adult teacher can assess the entering behavior of adults as to what conceptual knowledge they have prior to any instructional activity and what they can do with it (behavior).

A second advantage to utilizing conceptual statements, particularly when they are stated correctly, is that they offer clearly the direction, the materials, and the content of an individual learning unit. In the above-mentioned example on the welding concept, the direction that the adult teacher needs to take, the teaching materials involved, and the necessary content are very clear. Utilizing conceptual statements to describe the knowledge variable simplifies the instructional process because it actually makes explicit what needs to be done in order for the adult student to learn it and, thus, gain new behaviors.

A final advantage for specifying and utilizing these conceptual statements is that the adult teacher can translate these into overt behaviors that the adult student can display at the end of the instructional process; the terminal or new behavior is still the key concern. In other words the conceptual goals (content and knowledge) are compatible with behavioral goals (terminal behaviors) because the adult teacher can list the behaviors that the adult students should possess after they have interacted with their environment and have learned the content. The compatibility of behavior statements and conceptual statements makes the instructional process an easier task to perform. Further, as will be noted later in this chapter, it will aid significantly in organizing the content or substantive material in larger packages of instruction (that is, courses or modules of learning) for learning on the part of adult clients. This is important when adult

education curriculum workers begin to bring the larger
segments of learning into some organized and logical
form for easier learning on the part of their students.

Learning Unit and Procedures. Once the goals for a learning
unit have been carefully considered and clearly stated,
the adult instructor has an exact direction for the
development of the learning unit, be it a small or an
extended one. If the final behavior goals and, in turn,
the conceptual and instrumental goals are very explicit
the nature of the content and materials is right before
the instructor. If the instructor wishes to teach the
above-mentioned process concept on welding, the content
and materials are explicated. If the instructor wants
to have as a terminal performance the correct pronun-
ciation of twenty words in Spanish, the content and
materials are present. In all cases, then, the content
and materials are dictated by the goals previously
stated and not vice versa where content and materials
dictate the direction or goal of the learning experience.

The strategies and tasks are also dictated by the
goal statements. If the instructor wishes to achieve
applicative thinking (applying information) after basic
conceptual intake, then he/she must provide for the
concept formation by affording the adult student an
opportunity for basic interaction with the event or
object, and then pose tasks that will cause the student
to apply the information to new situations. If the
instructors want as a terminal performance the ability
to add numbers in two columns, then the strategy and
tasks are quite apparent. Again, in these cases the

nature of the tasks and strategies is dictated by the basic goal statements at the specific level.

In cases where more than one goal has been stated and in larger learning units, it will become necessary to organize and sequence the tasks to be presented to the adult students. Generally, and if necessary, the basic concept formation comes first before the adult students begin to think about and do things with the new concepts. Also, if several concepts are involved in a learning unit which lead to a principle of some sort, then organization must occur in the treatment of the concepts. Some logical order to the concepts will aid the students in their learning efforts. Adult instructors should think about and plan carefully the organization and sequence of tasks for the adult clients so as to eliminate haphazard treatments and to bring maximum potential to the learning experience.

An important consideration for developing a learning unit and one that ties in with entering behavior is to assess the amount and kind of direct sensory intake that has occurred prior to the new learning. For example, if would be difficult for adult students to use a micrometer and the concept of precise measurement in a vocational-technical class for some advanced work if they have not had direct contact with the instrument and what kinds of measurement it does. Students must have direct experience and contact with the instrument before any applicative use is possible. No amount of verbiage will accomplish this direct sensory input. It would also be difficult to work with a complex bill of sale if the adult students have never seen a real or simulated bill of sale first. However, if the students

have this basic input, then it is not necessary to feed
in through the senses this basic conceptual information.
A careful assessment is, therefore, required to ascertain what the students have actually perceived in their
experiences and interactions with their environment.

A final consideration in designing a learning unit
based on specified goals is that of time. Since all
adults in a classroom possess individual differences
and since the instructor's job is to teach all adult
students, it will be necessary to allow for these differences in terms of the time involved. Obviously, some
adults take longer with certain tasks than others and
the adult instructor must be aware of this fact when
designing learning units. If an expressed goal is important for all adult clients to achieve, then each
individual must have the time to so achieve. Most adults
can learn most things if given adequate time.

Presenting Learning Units. Under the guidance of the instructor the learning unit and the tasks, however simple or complex they may be, are presented to the adult
students. This is done, of course, in a classroom or
some similar learning situation and again is governed
by the nature of the goals and, in turn, the materials
and methods to achieve these goals. Whatever has been
specified as a terminal performance for the student
provides the direction for the adult instructor and
thus the instructor begins the interaction with the
adult clients regarding the content to be learned.

Since presenting the learning unit or the actual
teaching process is beyond the scope of this book,
little more will be stated here. Creating a positive

climate for adult learning and defining the appropriate strategies for the instructional process are discussed elsewhere in detail.[10] It must be kept in mind that different strategies may be necessary for all adults to learn. A major concern is that the adult instructor should keep apprised of the progress and the learning that adults are displaying in the learning situation. This leads to the final dimensions of the instructional process, that of the adult performance, feedback, and assessment of learning.

Adult Performance, Feedback, and Assessment. As adult students perform the various tasks in a learning unit, adult teachers and students must through a number of ways gather feedback to assess the level of learning, performance, and/or achievement. The goals or objectives of the learning unit should be so stated that the adult teacher can begin to look for the overt behavior or the products of the behavior that have resulted from the learning experience. The processes of evaluating adult learning, to be discussed in a later chapter, can be varied and many. The main point is that adult teachers must gather some evidence of the performance level of the adult learners. The need to gather evidence is apparent especially if the students are not performing as expected. If performance is not at the expected level, the instructor can quickly modify the goals, learning experiences, or perhaps presentations so that the students can proceed to achieve. If the terminal behavior of the students is congruous with the stated goals, then the students can proceed to new learning experiences. The final dimension of the instructional model then apprises the instructor of

where the adult learner is and what steps are necessary
to complete the learning unit or move to new learning.

CONTENT ORGANIZATION

Introduction. The content or substantive matter for adult
learning should be brought into some logical order so
that the learning process can proceed more effectively.
All adult learning involves some subject matter even
when it deals with some abstract idea or high-level
cognitive or affective process. As stated earlier we
deal with conceptual information about our world and/or
instrumental ideas as we program experiences for adult
learners. This conceptual information and the instrumental ideas are the subject matter or content for
adult learning.

Also suggested above was the explanation of the
basic compatibility and need for utilizing conceptual
information and objectives or goals together to insure
that selected substantive matter is acquired and that
appropriate behaviors in the three major domains are
achieved. This utilizing of the two major constructs
together in building instructional learning units or
packages strengthens the entire process because it
covers the subject matter to be learned and the resulting behaviors that will be formed after the adult
student interacts with the subject matter. With these
ideas in mind, some constructs can be advanced now
which will help bring organization to larger packages
of instruction.

Instructional Packages. As offered in chapter 4, the best
way to organize packages of instruction in various
sizes and lengths of time begins with utilizing the
intermediate goals as a guide. These goals provide the
direction for carefully defined packages of instruction
which could include a semester, a quarter, a course,
a module, and/or a year of concerted learning activity
for adults. By beginning with the intermediate level
of goal statements a more manageable package of instruction for adult students with more precise goals and
activities can be defined and organized which should
lead to better adult learning.

The beginning of course or program development comes
with some thinking about what kinds of behavior should
result from a major instructional package and what kinds
of substantive matter are required to elicit those
behaviors during the total instructional process. Some
direction can be gained in this effort by the general,
overriding goals of the institution or organization.
The goal statements at this level will indicate what
should happen as a result of an entire program for
adult students. Accompanying this direction source,
adult education curriculum workers can begin to survey
various sources and ascertain what kinds of behaviors
should result from a particular learning package. A
survey of the literature, a review of perceived adult
needs, a look at requirements of a job, business, profession, industry, and/or certification, an assessment
of other similar programs and courses, and some careful
thinking by concerned adult curriculum workers will
reveal what is important for adults to learn in a given
learning experience package. These sources lend considerable help in determining what should take place in a

larger learning endeavor, and the right questions have
to be asked at the outset. For example, a curriculum
builder might ask what kinds of behavior should result
from a beginning ceramics course, or a real estate
course, or a course using the computer in business. In
other words, the very general question should be asked,
"What kinds of things should adults need to know,
understand, use, do, appreciate, and value as a result
of this course or module of learning?" When all sources
are reviewed carefully, adult education curriculum
builders can then synthesize all ideas and determine
that which appears to be the very best terminal, intermediate goals for the adult learning package or module.

Figure 5.2, found on page 119 expresses in schematic
form the process of defining viable terminal goals or
behaviors to give direction to a meaningful package of
instruction for adults.

The defined goals or behaviors for a manageable
package of instruction should be expressed in all three
domains--cognitive, affective, and psychomotor--if all
are appropriate to the learning package. This is part
of the decision making process by adult curriculum
workers who determine what is important for adults to
learn in a given area. Further, these goals should be
expressed at the highest level in the hierarchy of the
three domains, as deemed appropriate for the area of
study, because they are the terminal goals for this
package of study. In other words, if applying information (third level, cognitive) is an ultimate goal
then it should be expressed for the course. If responding to stimuli (second level, affective) is sufficient, it should be stated. If some original creative
effort (seventh level, psychomotor) is seen as very

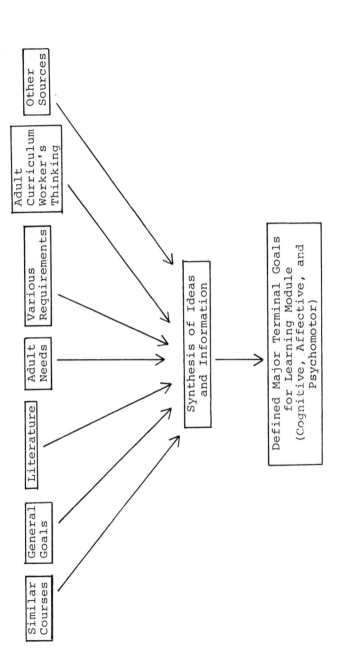

FIGURE 5.2 *Defining Terminal Goals for Unit of Instruction*

important in a given module of study, it too should be specified. In doing this, the appropriate highest-order goals are expressed as terminal behaviors for a course of study right at the outset and thus give the entire course a real sense of direction. Aiming for the top in the beginning is very important. The high-level goals then set the stage for further goal stating to meet these high-level ones.

Terminal Goals to Subordinate Goals--A Logic Tree. Once the high terminal goals for the module of adult learning are defined in the cognitive, affective, and psychomotor domains, if appropriate, the next step is to define subordinate goals that lead to the major statements. It is obvious because of the hierarchical nature of goals that before an adult student can apply information to new situations, he/she will have to know and understand the information first. The same holds true with the above example on original creation. The adult student must move up the psychomotor ladder through various experiences (and in turn achieve subordinate goals) before the adult will create something new and unique in a given area of study. In all cases the adult student will need to achieve lower goals, if not already done, before moving up to higher processes in the three domains. This will require the specification of lower goals which when achieved set the stage for the learning of higher-level goals. A kind of building-block approach is instituted and a tree results. The logical definition of these subordinate goals gives what might be called a logic tree.[11]

For example, if it is deemed important for the adult learners to be able to compare and contrast some

information (analysis, fourth level, cognitive) in a
given area of study, some sub-goals will have to be
defined that lead to knowledge acquisition, comprehension, and the application of the knowledge first.
In fact, there may be several kinds of information of
a conceptual nature that are necessary for the student
to compare and contrast in a given area of study. Thus,
the student must move up the cognitive ladder by knowing
(K), understanding (C), and applying (Ap) the kinds of
information which will then lead to the goal of analysis
(An).

A schematic representation of this might appear
thus:

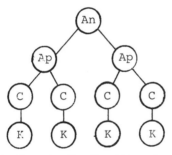

FIGURE 5.3 *Logic Tree in the Cognitive Domain*

In this case the adult learner will be required to
acquire four knowledge-level goals which then lead to
four comprehension goals. Also, the learner in using
the new knowledge with understanding will be asked to
apply them in two situations. Once application has been
achieved as a behavior, the adult learner will then
move to the analysis goal. In this example ten subordinate goals were defined leading to the major terminal
goal at the analysis level. This logic tree dealt only
with cognitive goals for a module of instruction.

In the psychomotor domain if adult curriculum builders see as important and define mechanism (fourth level, psychomotor) as the terminal required level for a
module of instruction whereby adult students should be
able to manipulate selected materials in a given content
area, they must then define sub-goals leading to this
important behavior. Within the hierarchy goals must be
defined at the perception (P), set (S), and guided
response (GR) levels which will prepare the adult to
move to the mechanism level (M) behaviorally. Perhaps
a module of instruction within the psychomotor domain
might appear as such:

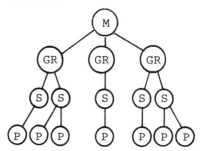

FIGURE 5.4 *Logic Tree in Psychomotor Domain*

Within this logical organization for a unit of study
in the psychomotor domain several sub-goals have to be
defined and achieved before moving to the terminal behavior. Several goals at the perception level and the
set level are required before moving to the guided response level. Once these are achieved satisfactorily
the three guided response level goals can prepare the
adult student to move to the terminal mechanism level.

Finally, running parallel to both the cognitive
and psychomotor domains should be a set of goal statements considering the affective development of adult

students. As suggested in an earlier chapter the affective domain comes into play when teaching cognitive and psychomotor goals regardless of their consideration or lack of consideration. It is better to define carefully some affective goals in the beginning and consciously strive for them during the entire length of the course or module of instruction. Consideration of these must be given during the definition stage so that they will be programmed in and, in turn, evaluated during the instructional process.

If for example adult education curriculum workers felt that a commitment to a process or procedure (valuing, third level, affective) is very important and should result from the formal study of a given area, they should then state it in the beginning. Once this terminal goal has been defined then sub-goals should also be defined to prepare the way for the terminal one.

An example of a logic tree for the affective domain using valuing (V) as the major goal with associated receiving (Rc) and responding (Rs) might appear as such:

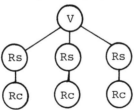

FIGURE 5.5 *Logic Tree in Affective Domain*

The above example is a very brief statement of goals, but it should be kept in mind that it takes time to foster learning in the affective domain. If a module of instruction in some adult education field could achieve the seven above-mentioned goals and bring the adult learner to a level of commitment for some important object or event, the module was probably very successful.

There will be numerous occasions when more than one major terminal goal will be specified in a single domain within a module of learning. And there will be occasions when both terminal cognitive and psychomotor goals will be specified in a module. Since the affective comes into play in all learning experiences these goals should receive attention and be placed into all learning modules.

The strength of using a logic tree concept in organizing the adult learning experiences is that it lays out exactly what needs to be covered in a package of instruction. The goals will be very explicit in terms of what all adult students should be able to do at the end of some major instructional course of study. Further, it gives direction as to what goals should be covered first in the vertical progression from simple to more complex and sophisticated behaviors on the part of adult learners. This brings organization and control over the entire instructional process and will eliminate the haphazard treatment of learning for adult students.

Finally, the logic tree concept for organizing the packages of learning for adults, as is noticed, emphasizes goal statements and not pure content or conceptual information. This is done because the job of adult educators is to help adult students form new behaviors and know when to use them, and not simply to acquire and store knowledge or content. The acid test for adult learners resulting from a learning experience is what new behaviors were formed and how they were used. Further, in utilizing goals the evaluation process is made easier in the fact that the instructors need only look for the new behaviors at the end of the instructional package. This adds strength to the entire endeavor because it builds in the final check of the learning experience.

Content or conceptual information, of course, is not being played down by the logic tree concept because adults learn by interacting with the objects and events of their environment, which is really content. The content, however, is tied in with the goal statements, as explicated earlier in this chapter, to bring more meaning to it and to the resulting learning experience.

Conceptual Information and Goals. In the instruction part of this chapter it was discussed how the content or conceptual information and goals were blended together and designed for the teaching act. The same notion holds true in organizing the learning experiences into a logic tree concept. In doing this it completes the interaction between the conceptual information and the goals and thus covers the subject matter to be learned and the resulting behaviors that will be formed after the learning experience. This must be planned for as adult curriculum workers define and organize the logic tree in the cognitive domain of behavior. In other words, when a behavioral goal is suggested as part of the tree the immediate interaction with content is implied and then defined to complete the learning experience. When considering both the conceptual information (CI) and the goals in the definition of a

learning package for adults, the resulting logic tree
might appear thus:

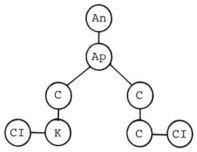

FIGURE 5.6 *Logic Tree with Conceptual Information*

Materials and Resources. If adult education curriculum
workers have carefully defined the learning goals of a
module of study and the associated conceptual information (concepts), the materials and related resources
should be apparent. It might behoove adult education
curriculum workers to define and list these potentially
required materials and resources in the module or
learning package so that they can be developed and/or
secured before the actual teaching takes place. Having
the materials and resources defined, listed, and ready
will strengthen the module of instruction and leave
nothing to chance.

Tasks and Strategies. Each goal or objective in the logic
tree along with associated conceptual information,
materials, and other resources is actually a specific
objective to be taught during the instructional phase.
The goal is thus the specific objective as defined in
the instructional model discussed earlier in this
chapter; this is where the actual teaching begins. Because of this the strategies and tasks to accomplish

these goals can be defined during the development of
the module of learning if this is deemed appropriate
by the curriculum workers making these decisions. If it
is felt that the individual instructor should have the
freedom to define the tasks and strategies for the
achievement of these objectives, then perhaps some
tentative or possible tasks and strategies might be
listed. However, if it is perceived as a tightly
structured course which all adult students in a given
program are required to take, or if it is part of a
recognized sequence of courses, or if it is developed
through programmed instructional techniques, then some
careful definition of the appropriate tasks and strategies would probably occur. Also, if a single instructor
teaches the course or module of learning some extensive
work on the tasks and strategies may be done by the
individual instructor.

Evaluation Statements and Procedures. Finally, within the
definition of an organized module of instruction for
adult learning there should be given some extensive
consideration as to the ways and means of measuring
or evaluating the growth that has taken place on the
part of the adult students.

Discussion on evaluation of adult student growth
will occur in the next chapter, so little will be stated
here. However, evaluation procedures must be built in
during the learning module development stage which will
determine if the individual adult student has acquired
the behaviors specified in the module. Without this
information adult educators cannot make any judgments
about adult student growth or the validity of the

learning experience. This evaluation process completes
the learning experience cycle for adult clients.

Other Considerations. Some final considerations regarding
the organization of a learning package should be mentioned in conclusion. First, the duration of the learning module and the setting in which it takes place are
contingent upon the goals to be achieved and the adult
learners involved. Different learning rates and motivations will cause a varied amount of time for the
learning to take place. This again argues for some individualization of experiences whenever necessary. The
setting--the classroom, the lab, the workshop or what-
ever--is dictated by the nature of the entire learning
experience. This is perhaps obvious, but provisions
must be made to ensure that the learning environment
matches the learning goals.

Consideration must be given initially to the level
of entering behavior required of the adult students
before entrance into the major package of learning.
Just like in the instructional act, entering behavior
must be compatible with the goals expressed or a break-
down in the learning will take place. Having adult
students in learning situations over their heads or,
at the other end, not challenging enough can do irrep-
arable harm to adult learning. Questions like what
previous learning experiences are required before entering this package or module and where does this package or module lead to next are critical ones for adult
education curriculum workers to consider. This is part
of the overall curriculum-building process for adult
learning. When the module or course is part of a sequential program for adults, careful coordination is

required. When it is a single learning experience the need for reviewing entering behavior is important. Also, it is important not to put the lid on learning by suggesting that this package is all there is to learn in a given subject area. Added experiences through reading, observations, participation and other means may be required in some cases. A total review of the learning module is thus required for successful adult learning.

This chapter has reviewed instructional ideas and constructs on organizing the substantive matter to be taught. Careful attention to these constructs and models will help adult education curriculum workers build better learning experiences for their clients. To complete the curriculum building process some attention has to be given to the evaluation process as related to adult learning. This is done in the following chapter.

6 / Evaluation

The term *evaluation* can mean many things to many educators. We hear of such processes as teacher evaluation, administrator evaluation, program and course evaluation, and other forms of evaluation. These processes are designed to gather information regarding the value of someone or something. The evaluation concept discussed in this chapter looks specifically at the evaluation of adult student learning as a result of the instructional experiences encountered in a daily learning unit, a course or module, and/or a program for adult learners in any adult learning center.

Evaluation is simply the process of gathering information and evidence to ascertain if the adult students have acquired the goals and objectives (behaviors) stated previously. In other words, evaluation checks to see how much adult learning has taken place in a given learning situation. It encompasses a great variety of methods beyond that of the usual paper and pencil examination, and it includes acquiring and processing the evidence needed to improve the adult student's learning and the teaching. It should be obvious that adult educators cannot operate in a precise and

professional manner without some evidence as to where
their adult students are in their learning experiences.

Three Levels. The root word of evaluation is value. The
process of evaluation checks the values involved. The
values involved in adult student learning are expressed
at the outset as goals. To keep the general curriculum
model consistent then, the evaluation process would
have to be geared to the goals expressed for adult
learning at the three different levels of specificity.
In other words, evaluation checks would have to be made
at the general level of goal statements, at the intermediate, and at the specific levels to be internally
consistent. Figure 6.1 illustrates the relationship
between the goals and the evaluation process.

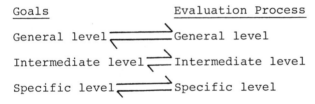

FIGURE 6.1 *Learning Goals and the Evaluation Process*

The horizontal, reversible arrows indicate the
interrelationship between the expressed goals and the
necessary evaluation process, a sort of checks and
balances concept. The vertical arrows indicate the
relationship of goals at three different levels and
the evaluation processes at three different levels.
Thus a close interaction between the goals and the
evaluation process at the three different levels must
be established to ensure that adult learning is being

assessed and that changes in strategies and even goals can be made as evidence indicates.

For each general-level goal that is specified for some adult program, an evaluation measure or measures should be identified and defined to assess if the goal was achieved and to what degree. The same would hold true for intermediate goals that are found in the learning modules and courses at that level. Finally, the evaluation measures should be established for the specific goals or objectives that are found in the instructional learning units and short-term learning experiences. In other words, some evaluation procedures should be defined for all goals set in the curriculum at different levels to see if, in fact, the desired behaviors were achieved. If the desired behaviors were acquired, then new learning can proceed. If not, then the feedback loop comes into play to ascertain why the desired behaviors were not acquired and what should be done. With the feedback system involved, the goals and the teaching and general learning experiences are under constant surveillance to ensure adequate adult learning. Without this evaluation information, intelligent decisions regarding adult learning cannot be made.

Three Domains. Since goals were probably specified in the three domains during the curriculum building and teaching phases, evaluation processes and procedures should be established to check the learning that took place in each of the three domains. Evaluation measures should be defined to assess the change in behavior that occurred in the cognitive domain, the affective domain, and the psychomotor domain. Evaluative measures are needed which look for the new behaviors or the products of the new behaviors that have resulted in adult learning in these three areas.

The key is, therefore, to specify clear, concise goals for learning and then specify some measures to see if the new behaviors are present after the learning experiences have taken place. If curriculum workers suggest that certain behaviors should be developed in a given module or program of study for adults and express these in fairly precise behavioral terms, then all the evaluation process consists of is to see if that particular behavior or product of the behavior is present after the adult learning experience has occurred. For example, in the cognitive domain, if an adult is expected to apply some knowledge to a new situation then the evaluation process would consist of seeing if the adult learner can apply the information in a new setting. Or if an adult was expected to argue for or against a position (affective), the evaluator so designs the process to see if, in fact, the adult can argue for or against a given proposition. Looking for the new behavior, as will be discussed later, can occur in a variety of evaluative situations. However, the fact remains that a given behavior, suggested as important for an adult to learn in any or all three domains, can be assessed by simply looking to see if the adult can display this behavior after some learning experiences have occurred. This sounds like a very simple process, which, of course, it is not. But the more carefully the goals are defined, the more individualized the instruction is, and the more precise the entire goal specification and instructional process is, the easier the measuring of the outcomes is. Several processes and techniques can aid in the entire endeavor.

Formative and Summative Evaluation Processes. To be internally consistent in the "checking" process of adult learning, some measures have to be instituted during the learning experience and some at the end. These two efforts will not only assist in the assessment of growth but will help in the entire feedback process.

A process of checking adult growth during the learning process is called formative evaluation. It derives its name from the fact that the evaluation comes during the "formative stage" of the learning experience. As opposed to summative evaluation, it occurs during the process while instruction is still fluid and susceptible to modification. It intervenes during the formation of behaviors--not at the end--and can provide evidence for remediation or immediate treatment. It can pinpoint the tasks that are not accomplished and mastered, and can assist in the pacing of adult students and their learning experiences. It is in effect the feedback loop during the teaching-learning process.

It should be kept in mind that formative evaluation reveals less generalizable evidence and less transferable outcomes because the entire learning experience has not been completed. But it can give evidence during the learning experiences before it is too late (at the end) to modify the instruction.

Formative evaluation is an effective process for smaller independent units of instruction such as those involved in the instructional learning unit described

in the previous chapter. It can give some evidence as
to the quality of adult learning which in turn can
cause modification in the goals, learning unit, or
teaching if need be. It is also effective in various
parts and divisions of courses and programs. As Bloom,
Hastings, and Madaus suggest:

Most fundamental to the use of formative evaluation is
the selection of a unit of learning. Within a course
or education program there are parts or divisions
which have a separable existence such that they can,
at least for analytic purposes, be considered in
relative isolation from other parts. While these parts
may be interrelated in various ways so that the
learning (or level of learning) of one part has consequences for the learning of others, it is still possible
to consider the parts separately.[1]

The key to using the formative process for evaluation, like other phases of curriculum building, is
deciding when it is important to gather some evidence
on adult learning while it is occurring. This decision-
making process should include the nature of the learning
units and/or modules, their relationship to larger
packages of instruction and goals, the kinds of evidence
needed, and, of course, the kinds of goals specified
at the outset of the instructional package. A basic
question is what kinds of evidence are needed and when
are they needed during the learning experiences?

If one utilizes a logic tree, discussed in chapter
5, to bring organization to the learning experiences
for adults, formative evaluation will probably occur
as each behavior is learned (or not learned) as instruction moves up the tree itself. Movement up the tree
cannot occur until certain behaviors are acquired and
formative evaluation can give the needed evidence for
such decision-making. This evaluation process should

probably be built in during the construction of the learning unit. The formative process can also be employed by instructors at their discretion during any phase of the instructional activity. Finally, formative evaluation can be built in at the end of the module or tree of behaviors if this is a fairly discreet part of a larger learning package. In any case, the use of formative evaluation must receive attention at the curriculum-building stage so that adequate provisions are made to check adult learning during the process.

Summative evaluation, as opposed to formative, is geared toward a much more general assessment of the degree to which adult learners have acquired larger outcomes over an entire course, module, or some substantial part of them. This process looks at the broad ability of an adult learner to do or know something as a result of a larger package of instructional experiences. As the name suggests, it is kind of a summation of the kinds of learning that have taken place in a course or module of study. A broader level of generalization and transferability of behaviors can be ascertained through a summative approach to evaluation. It has and can be used for grading and reporting of learner progress in a given major learning experience. And, it also has and can be used for the licensing and certification of adults for given areas of study. Finally, it should indicate how much learning took place at the end of a major segment of instruction. Whereas formative measures are shorter and more frequent in nature, summative measures are generally longer and less frequent. This is because summative evaluation places the emphasis on collecting more information to give a more

global view of the adult learner's behavior after a
lengthy learning experience.

Several decisions are required by adult education
curriculum workers in using the summative process in
evaluating learning goals. One decision rests with
where summative evaluation may be required or necessary
before the very end of a major course or module of
learning. For example, just because two or three general
tests have been given in most subject areas previously
is no reason why this concept should continue. The
question should be, are there some logical and necessary
places in a major course of instruction to gather cumu-
lative evidence regarding the general growth and
learning in adults? If this is then apparent some
summative evaluation can be instituted to evaluate the
overall learning and growth to a given point in the
course or module.

Also falling within the decision-making domain of
curriculum workers relative to summative evaluation is
the problem that some determination as to the kinds of
evidence desired to assess the total growth of adults
must be made. It would be difficult, lengthy, and
probably unnecessary to check to see if all of the
defined behaviors were gained by the adult learners in
a major course of study. Therefore, some sampling of
the prescribed behaviors will help adult educators
determine if mastery of major goals was achieved.
Since there is a building block of hierarchical approach
to the logic tree, the major goals for a module or
course of study will be the areas to assess in a summative manner. Sampling of these behaviors may provide
evidence sufficient to ascertain the total learning,

and thus assessing all of the given behaviors may not be necessary. This decision must be made by the curriculum workers involved.

Internal-External Means. Besides the important processes of formative and summative evaluation, a couple of other measurement concepts should be brought to adult educators' attention when involvement in the curriculum-building process is taking place. These will help when deciding upon the means of gathering evidence for determining adult learning.

Internal means are procedures that are developed locally usually to gather evidence that will determine if the goals were achieved based on some behavioral-criterion reference previously specified. External means are measures of gaining evidence based on the use of some standardized or norm-referenced measure. The internal or criterion-referenced measure can be used to check the growth of an individual adult against the behavioral goals specifically identified for him or her. The external or norm-referenced measure would give some evidence as to how the adult learner compares with and is doing based on some standard or norm set empirically for people in the same general category. Internal or really teacher-made measures check the growth of the individual based on some criteria established for the individual where external or usually standardized tests compare the individual with a given norm. The use of either or both measures is, of course, dependent on the kinds of goals established at the outset.

If, for example, the goal for all beginning adult

basic education students was established as having them
read at the third-grade level as a result of a beginning
course or module on reading instruction, then some
standardized measure should be employed to check the
reading growth of participating adults. After completion
of the course the adults would be given a standardized
reading test to see what achievement had occurred and
if the goal was met. However, if the goal was to have
adult students describe the processes involved in
getting a bill into law, some internally developed
measures would be instituted to see if the students
possessed this knowledge. The teacher-made measure
probably would require the adult students to write on
paper how the process occurs.

Although these internal-external ideas are probably
obvious to adult educators, there are still implications
for their use in curriculum building. One must decide
upon the better method for collecting evidence at the
end of some learning experience based, of course, on
the goal specification. During the curriculum-building
process some thought must be given and procedures should
be specified as to how evidence of learning will be
measured. This should not be omitted or left to chance.

Another critical decision deals with the standards
of acceptable performance in a given area of study. In
other words what level of performance in a given
learning experience should the adult learner achieve
to insure competency, or to pass the experience, or to
achieve certification, a license, or a diploma, or to
move to the next level of study, or to just get "a
good grade?" Should an adult learner perform a given
behavior correctly 100 percent of the time, 90 percent

of the time, or 75 percent of the time? Should an adult student get at least a 75 on a standardized test of some sort to move to the next level of instruction, or receive a passing grade, or receive some sort of certification or license? If some level of performance is important and necessary in a given area of study, the level should receive serious consideration and be specified by the appropriate curriculum workers. These levels or standards of performance may be specified in the goals and thus are explicit from the start. If they are not, and if standards are important, they can then be instituted during the evaluation process. The former is must more preferable.

Standards sometimes are established outside the domain of the adult education center by other agencies. A passing grade on the General Educational Development test (GED) is an example. Other standards for licensing and certification may be specified from without in a number of areas. Adult education curriculum workers should be apprised of these when building and measuring curriculum experiences.

Other standards may be implied because of the very nature of the area of study. In an adult vocational typing course, a selected standard for typing competency may be dictated by the fact that people seeking good jobs in secretarial positions may have to type sixty words a minute with perhaps only two mistakes permitted. Therefore, adult students would have to measure up to that standard in order to secure appropriate employment. Also, an adult student in an auto mechanics course may be expected to fix the brakes of an automobile correctly 100 percent of the time to get and sustain a job as a

mechanic, or an adult student in a nurse's aide class
may be expected to administer the correct dosage of
medication to a patient 100 percent of the time like-
wise to get and sustain a position in that area. These
standards are dictated by the nature of the study.

Other areas of study in adult education may not
have very explicit or implicit outside standards to
judge the competency of learning on the part of adult
clients. In these areas curriculum workers must draw
upon experience or the literature to suggest some
standards if they are deemed appropriate.

Some Tools for Evidence Gathering. Again, the goals set the
stage for the various evaluation measures that will be
instituted to ascertain what learning has taken place
during and at the end of a given learning experience.
And, goals can be specified in various domains and at
many different levels. Therefore, it is highly probable
that numerous tools will be required to assess the
resulting learning in the various domains at various
levels.

The resulting behavior from a learning experience
may not be in evidence directly. It may be in the form
of a behavioral state; that is, it may be within the
individual adult learner and not overt. Therefore, some
product of the new behavior will have to be displayed
before one can say if the behavior was actually learned.
Displaying the new behavior or product of behavior can
come in many forms, the most common of which being,
of course, through a paper and pencil effort. But overt
behavior and products of behavior can be seen in other
ways too.

For the paper and pencil measurement effort numerous tools are available. The standardized test and the teacher-made objective test and essay test (or combinations) are useful tools. The use of workbooks and worksheets can give evidence of the growth of adult learners. A written self-evaluation will give evidence as to changes in behavior, although caution should be used when checking the affective domain with this tool. Adults could state on paper that some significant affective changes have occurred in them, but this may not be the case. Also, adult educators can get some assessment evidence by looking for the application in written form of the learned behaviors to other areas of study. This could happen by reviewing an adult's work in some similar content areas and in any future work where the learned behaviors should be evident.

Adults can convey newly learned behaviors in an oral fashion too. This can happen through oral tests, oral reports, discussions, and conferences where evidence can be gained regarding growth in the three major domains.

Finally, observations of all sorts are effective tools to gain evidence as to the amount and quality of adult learning that has occurred during both formative and summative periods of evaluation. In fact, the observation process is a very effective tool to view new behaviors or the products of the new behaviors, and should not be overlooked.

The use of the above-mentioned tools or others like them to gather evaluative evidence is again part of the decision-making process of adult education curriculum workers. Generally, the kind of terminal

behavior that is expected from instruction will dictate
the kind of tool needed for evaluation purposes, and
in many cases more than one tool may be required.

7 / Some Application Ideas

The models, constructs, and ideas found in the previous chapters have been presented in quite a generalized manner. This has been done on purpose because of the very diverse nature of educating adults in various settings. Adult educators are responsible for building programs and courses for the highly educated, the poorly educated, and those in between. They must develop experiences for low-economic-status adults up to those who may be quite affluent. They must develop experiences to teach basic literacy skills and very highly technical skills to adults. They must work with young adults and senior citizens. They teach adults in very brief learning situations or in long-term programs. They teach adults recreational and leisure experiences and they teach adults very important ideas related directly to their employment possibilities. They teach highly motivated adults and those who are quite unmotivated. And the content or subject matter is as highly varied as the setting in which the learning takes place.

All of these factors would suggest that curriculum building for adult learning is not an easy job because of the nature of the client and the tasks confronting

adult educators. Thus, these factors lend themselves
to discussing curriculum building in very general terms
and to leaving the application of ideas up to adult
curriculum workers in their individual adult learning
situations.

However, even with the extreme variability and di-
versity associated with adult learning, some guidelines
for applying the general ideas and model are available.
Many of these guidelines are dependent on the nature
of the adult curriculum workers' mission and task. Each
model and construct discussed previously will have
meaning if applied in the correct adult learning setting.
Again, decisions are required on the part of adult educators as to when to use the various constructs and
models.

Program and Mission. The general learning program in
which adult educators find themselves is a critical
concern to using the general curriculum model or parts
of it for adult learning, and the mission and/or the
kinds of adult learning that are desirable and are
required within the general setting are of vital importance.

Working with adults and their learning experiences
can involve long-term efforts or very short-lived experiences; it can include very complete, comprehensive
experiences or those of an in-and-out nature. And it
can involve and in fact suggest that different kinds
of learning will take place within an adult learning
situation. For those with broader, longer-range programs with rather definite learning experiences offered,
some guides to application may be defined.

Adult institutions such as community colleges, adult vocational-technical centers, correctional centers, and adult basic education schools have longer-range programs for enhancing adult behaviors. Other organizations which previously have not been associated with the formal education of adults such as industry, business, hospitals, and other social service units have generally defined long-range programs for the education, training, and retraining of their adult clients to enhance their people's behaviors and perhaps the output of the various organizations. For these institutions and organizations a longer and broader view of adult learning is probably of utmost concern to the involved adult educators. These adult educators are interested in a variety of behaviors being learned by the adult clients which can in turn lead to more productive outcomes for the individual and in many cases the organizations. For these institutions and organizations a more global and comprehensive view of curriculum building should be envisioned. A philosophy or rationale for the learning of adults within the learning center should be established. It should specify what is important for adult learning, training, and retraining. It should make clear what philosophically should be established in the actual curriculum design and why. It should provide the base or foundation for all the goals, instruction, and evaluation processes that are important to adults who will be learning many things within the institution or organization. It will in fact provide a philosophical measure of accountability for the learning experiences that are taking place within the learning establishment.

The rationale model advanced in chapter 2 should have direct meaning for the programs of various adult education institutions identified above. Consideration of all the identified variables within the model is important so that a total base for adult learning can be established.

For the other organizations identified above perhaps the total rationale model does not have complete application. However, selected parts of it should be given consideration in order to establish a foundation for the organized learning experiences under the direction of the organization. Other areas such as "Needs of the Organization" might be identified and addressed in these instances. In any case a more coherent and consistent set of learning experiences can be developed when a clear and concise philosophical base is established in the beginning. In the case of both institutions and organizations with total programs a more coordinated program can evolve with more control over the learning situation if careful thought is given to the early specification of a philosophical curriculum base.

For major program efforts in any adult learning area constant concern for the "outside political forces" playing upon the local curriculum must be established and maintained at all times. Adult education curriculum workers must be apprised of those forces from outside which in effect establish policy in the local program. Requirements for certification and licensing are important. New program specifications and changes in requirements by professional associations, societies, unions, and accrediting agencies must be attended to. Policy that is "established" by

textbooks, other materials, and standardized tests is
critical. Governmental regulations must receive attention by curriculum builders. Other forces or factors
that have a direct bearing on adult learning that come
from outside the local decision-making apparatus also
must be considered, so that the most productive thinking and curriculum building effort can take place by
adult educators.

Finally, within the domain of major, long-range
program efforts, consideration should be afforded to
establishing goals at the three levels of specificity--
general, intermediate, and specific. Although most
curriculum-building activity occurs as a result of
establishing goals at the intermediate and specific
levels, some overriding direction for the entire program for educating, training, and retraining adults
should be specified at the general, abstract level.
This level sets the direction for the entire program
effort and serves as a constant referent for all other
learning activities. Goals establish what goes on in
the rest of the curriculum, and general goals give
direction to the other levels of goal statement in
program development work. All else should be contingent
upon this level of goal statements as it brings coordination to total training and educational efforts.
Adult educators who deal with larger, organized programs must give thought and action to general goals
for the ultimate direction a program or programs will
take. This should happen even if some of the training
and educational efforts might be perceived as rather
piecemeal and isolated in nature. With general goals
specified more coordination will develop.

It should be obvious that the other major elements of the curriculum model--instruction and content organization and evaluation--have to receive careful attention in major program efforts. Adult education curriculum workers must design instruction and organize the substantive matter for effective learning, and they must define measures to evaluate the kinds of learning that take place in an adult learning center. The models and constructs offered in these major areas should have considerable meaning and application by curriculum workers.

It is therefore suggested that, within those adult learning centers where total programs are offered to enhance adult learning and growth in a variety of ways, the entire curriculum model should have direct application in developing and building effective learning programs. The use of complete models should ensure that coordinated and useful learning experiences are developed for the adults in the various programs.

For those adult learning center situations where just a few courses are offered or where isolated experiences are given, the use of the complete model may be inappropriate. There may be no need to build a complete rationale for a program or series of programs when none exists. This would not preclude, of course, any serious thought in the general area. However, some thought, organization, and development of goals at the intermediate level and specific level are critical. Further, considerable attention must be focused on the instructional processes and content organization since the teaching act would still be a vital part of adult learning. The evaluation process, too, is important to

check the amount of learning that has taken place.
Perhaps in adult learning centers where few or isolated courses are presented it might be very important
to organize the learning experiences very carefully to
ensure that maximum learning can take place. Careful
curriculum-building activity is definitely required
here.

Regardless of the nature of the programs or courses
offered and the basic mission of the adult learning
center involved, more precise curriculum work should
ensure better learning on the parts of the adult
clients. This should be the overriding purpose of any
adult learning center.

Step-By-Step Approach. To further implement the general
curriculum model for adult learning a step-by-step
approach is recommended. That is, adult education curriculum workers should begin with the philosophical
base for establishing and maintaining adult learning
efforts. Consideration of the important variables
identified will lead to a foundation on which to build
significant learning experiences for all adult clients.
If some rationale is currently present within the
local learning center, then a careful review of it
should be made. The rationale should be kept up-to-date
because it provides the underpinnings on which all
else is built. Again, it provides philosophical accountability for what takes place in any adult learning
program.

The next step would be to review carefully the
forces or factors from outside the local learning
situation to see which ones have meaning and may

impinge upon the local program. It is very important
for adult education curriculum workers to keep themselves apprised of all forces that affect the welfare
of their adult clients. Without this awareness very
ineffective programs can be developed.

After a philosophical base is developed and critical outside forces are identified and considered, the
next step involves the definition of goals to guide
long-range programs and, if deemed appropriate, goals
for courses, modules, or other packages of instruction.
At the outset some consensus must be reached as to
what the major goals to govern programs should be;
these again give direction for the programs. Then using
these as referents, some goals may be specified for
the intermediate level which gives direction to the
manageable learning packages. This phase of curriculum
building deserves the very best thinking and review by
curriculum workers because all other activities are
contingent upon goals.

Following the definition of goals, attention is
given to organizing the content to be learned and the
instructional process. The identification of intermediate goals gives direction to organizing the content.
Ultimate terminal goals are placed at the top of the
logic tree followed by sub-goals that lead to the
higher-order goals in the three major domains. Conceptual information, materials, and procedures are
tied in with various goals in the tree to make a
unified package of instruction for adult learners.
This package can be taught to adults utilizing the
instructional model advanced earlier. At this time
some formative procedures for evaluating learning can

be established. This will give an indication as to whether learning is taking place during the process. Finally, summative procedures should be established based on the specified goals to determine the quality and quantity of learning that has occurred at the end of the course, module, or some major segment of them.

A methodical approach utilizing the various models and constructs should result in a coherent and consistent set of learning experiences for adult learners. It is not the purpose of this book to discuss actual processes and uses of people in the process of curriculum building. This writer has done this elsewhere.[1] The purpose is to identify some guides to curriculum organization which should aid curriculum workers, whoever they might be, to structure better programs for adult learning. These guides plus critical thinking and investigation by adult education curriculum workers should result in this goal.

NOTES   SELECTED BIBLIOGRAPHY   INDEX

Notes

CHAPTER 1. INTRODUCTION

1. John R. Verduin, Jr., Harry G. Miller, and
Charles E. Greer, Adults Teaching Adults: Principles
and Strategies (Austin, Tex.: Learning Concepts, 1977),
p. 31.

2. Ralph W. Tyler, Principles of Curriculum and
Instruction (Chicago: University of Chicago Press,
1950).

3. Hilda Taba, Curriculum Development: Theory and
Practice (New York: Harcourt, Brace and World, 1962).

CHAPTER 2. RATIONALE

1. George F. Kneller, Foundations of Education
(New York: John Wiley and Sons, 1963).

2. J.W. Getzels and Herbert A. Thelen, "The Classroom Group As a Unique Social System," in 56th Yearbook,
The Dynamics of Instructional Groups: Part II (Chicago:
National Society for the Study of Education, 1960),
pp. 53-82.

3. See John R. Verduin, Jr., Conceptual Models in
Teacher Education: An Approach to Teaching and Learning
(Washington, D.C.: American Association of Colleges for
Teacher Education, 1967), chap. 7.

4. Ibid., p. 62.

CHAPTER 3. OUTSIDE POLITICAL FORCES

1. Michael W. Kirst and Decker F. Walker, "An Analysis of Curriculum Policy-Making," Review of

Educational Research 41, no. 5 (Dec. 1971): 482.
    2. Ibid., pp. 479-509.
    3. Ibid., p. 488.

CHAPTER 4. CURRICULUM GOALS
    1. Robert F. Mager, Preparing Objectives for Pro-
grammed Instruction (San Francisco: Fearon Publishers,
1961), p. 3.
    2. David R. Krathwohl, "Stating Objectives Appro-
priately for Program, for Curriculum, and for Instructional Materials Development," Journal of Teacher
Education 16, no. 1 (March 1965): 83-92.
    3. Ibid., p. 86.
    4. For a discussion, see Harold Spears, "Kappans
Ponder the Goals of Education," Phi Delta Kappan 55,
no. 1 (Sept. 1973): 29-32.
    5. Benjamin S. Bloom et al., Taxonomy of Educational
Objectives. The Classification of Educational Goals,
Handbook 1: Cognitive Domain (New York: David McKay,
1956), from appendix pages 201-7, copyright c 1956 by
Longman Inc., reprinted with permission of Longman.
    6. Newton S. Metfessel, William B. Michael, and
Donald A. Kirsner, "Instrumentation of Bloom's and
Krathwohl's Taxonomies for the Writing of Educational
Objectives," Psychology in the Schools 6, no. 3
(July 1969): 228-29.
    7. David R. Krathwohl, Benjamin S. Bloom, and
Bertram B. Masia, Taxonomy of Educational Objectives.
The Classification of Educational Goals, Handbook 2:
Affective Domain (New York: David McKay, 1964), from
Appendix A, pp. 176-85, copyright c 1964 by Longman,
Inc., reprinted with permission of Longman.
    8. Metfessel, Michael, and Kirsner, "Instrumentation
of Bloom's and Krathwohl's Taxonomies for the Writing
of Educational Objectives," pp. 230-31.
    9. Elizabeth J. Simpson, "The Classification of
Educational Objectives in the Psychomotor Domain," in
The Psychomotor Domain, Floyd Urbach, ed. (Washington,
D.C.: Gryphon House, 1972), pp. 43-56.
    10. Ibid.
    11. Verduin, Miller, and Greer, Adults Teaching
Adults.
    12. Ibid., p. 74.
    13. Ibid., pp. 74-75.
    14. Ibid., pp. 75-76.
    15. Ibid., p. 76.

16. Ibid., p. 77.
17. Ibid., pp. 77-78.
18. Wayne Dumas, "Can We Be Behaviorists and Humanists Too?" Educational Forum 37, no. 3 (March 1973): 303-6.

CHAPTER 5. INSTRUCTION AND CONTENT ORGANIZATION

1. Verduin, Miller, and Greer, Adults Teaching Adults, p. 51.
2. N. L. Gage, ed., Handbook on Research on Teaching (Chicago: Rand McNally and Co., 1963), p. 96.
3. John P. De Cecco and William R. Crawford, The Psychology of Learning and Instruction: Educational Psychology, 2nd ed. (Englewood Cliffs, N.J.: Prentice-Hall, 1974), p. 48.
4. Ibid., pp. 48-49.
5. Asahel D. Woodruff, "Putting Subject Matter into Conceptual Form" (Paper prepared for TEAM Project [which Project was sponsored by The American Association of Colleges for Teacher Education], Washington, D.C., Feb. 6, 1964).
6. Ibid.
7. Ibid.
8. Verduin, Miller, and Greer, Adults Teaching Adults, p. 55.
9. Ibid., p. 55.
10. Ibid.
11. Albert E. Hickey and John M. Newton, The Logical Basis of Teaching: I. The Effect of Sub-concept Sequence on Learning (Newburyport, Mass.: ENTELEK, Jan. 1964).

CHAPTER 6. EVALUATION

1. Benjamin S. Bloom, J. Thomas Hastings, and George F. Madaus, Handbook on Formative and Summative Evaluation of Student Learning (New York: McGraw-Hill Book Co., 1971), p. 118.

CHAPTER 7. SOME APPLICATION IDEAS

1. John R. Verduin, Jr., Cooperative Curriculum Improvement (Englewood Cliffs, N.J.: Prentice-Hall, 1967).

Selected Bibliography

Adams, D. A. Review and Synthesis of Research Concerning Adult Vocational and Technical Education. Columbus, Ohio: ERIC Clearinghouse on Vocational and Technical Education, 1972.

Alpenfels, Ethel J. Families of the Future. Ames, Iowa: Iowa State University Press, 1971.

Anderson, Scarvia B., Samuel Ball, Richard T. Murphy, and Associates. Encyclopedia of Educational Evaluation. San Francisco: Jossey-Bass, 1975.

Atkin, J. M. "Behavioral Objectives in Curriculum Design: A Cautionary Note." Science Teacher 35, no. 5 (May 1968): 27-30.

Axford, Roger W. Adult Education: The Open Door. Scranton, Pa.: International Textbook Co., 1969.

Barker, P. B., and P. Schoggen, eds. Qualities of Community Life. San Francisco: Jossey-Bass, 1973.

Belbin, Eunice, and R. M. Belbin. Problems in Adult Retraining. London: Heinemann, 1972.

Benaim, S., and I. Allen, eds. The Middle Years. London: T. V. Publications, 1967.

Bergevin, Paul, and J. McKinley. Participation Training for Adult Education. New York: Seabury Press, 1963.

Bergevin, Paul, D. Morris, and Robert Smith. Adult Education Procedures. New York: Seabury Press, 1963.

Bischof, Ledford J. Adult Psychology. New York: Harper and Row, 1969.

Block, Jack, and Norma Haan. Lives Through Time. Berkeley, Calif.: Bancroft Books, 1971.

Bloom, Benjamin S., J. Thomas Hastings, and George F. Madaus. Handbook on Formative and Summative Evaluation of Student Learning. New York: McGraw-Hill Book Co., 1971.

Bloom, Benjamin S., Max D. Engelhart, Edward J. Furst, Walter H. Hill, and David R. Krathwohl. Taxonomy of Educational Objectives; The Classification of Educational Goals, Handbook 1: Cognitive Domain. New York: David McKay, 1956.

Boone, E. J., and E. H. Quinn. Curriculum Development in Adult Basic Education. Chicago: Follett Education Corporation, 1967.

Botwinick, Jack. Aging and Behavior. New York: Springer, 1973.

Britton, J. H., and J. O. Britton. Personality Changes in Aging. New York: Springer, 1972.

Brooke, W. M., ed. Adult Basic Education. Toronto: New Press, 1972.

Brotman, H. B. Facts and Figures on Older Americans. Washington, D.C.: U.S. Department of Health, Education, and Welfare, 1972.

Burns, Richard W. "The Theory of Expressing Objectives." Educational Technology 7, no. 20 (October 1967): 1-3.

Buros, Oscar K., ed. The Sixth Mental Measurements Yearbook. Highland Park, N.J.: Gryphon Press, 1965.

Burrichter, A. W., and Curtis Ulmer, eds. Special Techniques That Work in Teaching the Culturally Deprived. Englewood Cliffs, N.J.: Prentice-Hall, 1972.

Byrn, Darrie, ed. Evaluation in Extension. U.S. Federal Extension Service, Division of Extension Research and Training. Topeka: H. M. Ives, 1959.

Cass, Angelica W. Basic Education for Adults. New York: Association Press, 1971.

Clark, D. Cecil. Using Instructional Objectives in Teaching. Glenview, Ill.: Scott, Foresman and Co., 1972.

Cross, P., and J. Valley, eds. Planning Non-traditional Programs: An Analysis of the Issues for Postsecondary Education. San Francisco: Jossey-Bass, 1974.

De Cecco, John P., and William R. Crawford. The Psychology of Learning and Instruction: Educational Psychology. 2d ed. Englewood Cliffs, N.J.: Prentice-Hall, 1974.

Dickinson, G. Teaching Adults: A Handbook for Instructors. Toronto: New Press, 1973.

Dubin, Samuel and Morris Okun. "Implications of Learning Theories for Adult Instruction." Adult Education 24, no. 1 (Fall 1973): 3-19.

Dumas, Wayne. "Can We Be Behaviorists and Humanists Too?" Educational Forum 37, no. 3 (March 1973): 303-6.

Ennis, Robert. Logic in Teaching. Englewood Cliffs, N.J.: Prentice-Hall, 1969.

Field, Minna. The Aged, The Family, and The Community. New York: Columbia University Press, 1972.

Franzblau, Rose N. The Middle Generation. New York: Holt, Rinehart and Winston, 1971.

Gage, N. L., ed. Handbook on Research on Teaching. Chicago: Rand McNally and Co., 1963.

Getzels, J. W., and Herbert A. Thelen. "The Classroom Group As a Unique Social System." In 56th Yearbook, The Dynamics of Instructional Groups: Part II. Chicago: National Society for the Study of Education, 1960. Pp 53-82.

Goldhammer, Keith. "The Proper Federal Role in Education Today." Educational Leadership 35, no. 5 (February 1978): 350-53.

Gronlund, Norman E. Measurement and Evaluation in Teaching. 3d ed. New York: Macmillan Co., 1975.

Goss, Ronald. The Lifelong Learner. New York: Simon and Schuster, 1977.

Grotelueschen, Arden D., Dennis Gooler, and Alan G. Knox. Evaluation in Adult Basic Education: How and Why. Urbana: Office for the Study of Continuing Professional Education, University of Illinois, 1972.

Grotelueschen, Arden D., Dennis Gooler, Alan Knox, Stephen Kemmis, Irene Sowsly, and Kathleen Brophy. An Evaluation Planner. Urbana: Office for the Study of Continuing Professional Education, University of Illinois, 1974.

Hall, Kenneth D., and Virginia Bunson. "What About Curriculum Reform at the State Level?" Educational Leadership 35, no. 5 (February 1978): 342-49.

Harrington, Fred H. The Future of Adult Education. San Francisco: Jossey-Bass, 1976.

Harris, L., and Associates. Myth and Reality of Aging in America. Washington, D.C.: National Council on Aging, 1975.

Harrow, Anita J. A Taxonomy of the Psychomotor Domain: A Guide for Developing Behavioral Objectives. New York: David Mckay, 1972.

Hickey, Albert E., and John M. Newton. The Logical Basis of Teaching: I. The Effect of Sub-concept Sequence on Learning. Newburyport, Mass.: ENTELEK, January 1964.

Hiemstra, Roger. Lifelong Learning. Lincoln Neb.: Professional Educators Publications, 1976.

Hiestand, Dale L. Changing Careers After Thirty-Five. New York: Columbia University Press, 1971.

Joyce, Bruce, and M. Weil. Models of Teaching. Englewood Cliffs, N.J.: Prentice-Hall, 1972.

Kalish, Richard A. Late Adulthood: Perspectives on Human Development. Monterey, Calif.: Books-Cile, 1975.

Kapfer, Philip G. "Behavioral Objectives in the Cognitive and Affective Domains." Educational Technology 8, no. 11 (June 1968): 11-13.

Kenneke, L. J., Dennis Nystrom, and Ronald W. Stadt. Planning and Organizing Career Curricula: Articulated Education. New York: Howard W. Sams and Co., 1973.

Kibler, Robert J., L. Barker, and David T. Miles. Behavioral Objectives and Instruction. Boston: Allyn and Bacon, 1970.

Kidd, J. R. How Adults Learn. Rev. ed. New York: Association Press, 1973.

Kirst, Michael W., and Decker F. Walker. "An Analysis of Curriculum Policy-Making." Review of Educational Research 41, no. 5 (December 1971): 479-507.

Klevins, Chester, ed. Materials and Methods in Adult Education. New York: Klevins Publications, 1972.

Kneller, George F. Foundations of Education. New York: John Wiley and Sons, 1963.

Knowles, Malcolm S. The Adult Learner: A Neglected Species. Houston: Gulf Publishing Co., 1973.

____. The Modern Practice of Adult Education. New York: Association Press, 1970.

Knowles, Malcolm S., ed. Handbook of Adult Education. Chicago: Adult Education Association of the U.S.A., 1960.

Knox, Alan B. Adult Development and Learning. San Francisco: Jossey-Bass, 1977.

Krathwohl, David R. "Stating Objectives Appropriately for Program, for Curriculum, and for Instructional Materials Development." Journal of Teacher Education 16, no. 1 (March 1965): 83-92.

____. "The Taxonomy of Educational Objectives: Its Use in Curriculum Building." In C. M. Lindvall, ed., Defining Educational Objectives. Pittsburgh: University of Pittsburgh Press, 1964. Pp. 19-36.

Krathwohl, David R., Benjamin S. Bloom, and Bertram B.
Masia. Taxonomy of Educational Objectives; The
Classification of Educational Goals, Handbook 2:
Affective Domain. New York: David McKay, 1964.

Krietlow, B. W. Educating the Adult Educator; Part I:
Concepts for the Curriculum. Madison: University
of Wisconsin-Madison, March 1965.

Kuhler, R. G., ed. Psychological Backgrounds of Adult
Education. New York: Association Press, 1970.

Kurland, Norman D. "A National Strategy for Lifelong
Learning." Phi Delta Kappa 59, no. 6 (February
1978): 385-89.

Land, George T. Grow or Die. New York: Random House,
1973.

Lenyand, Elinore, and Marjorie H. Shaevitz. So You Want
to Go Back to School: Facing the Realities of Re-
entry. New York: McGraw-Hill Book Co., 1977.

Le Shan, Eda. The Wonderful Crisis of Middle Age. New
York: Random House, 1973.

Lidz, Theodore. The Person: His Development Throughout
the Life Cycle. New York: Basic Books, 1968.

Lloyd, J. H. A Handbook for Teachers of Adults. Washington, D.C.: Federal City College, 1972.

Long, H. B. The Physiology of Aging: How It Affects
Learning. Englewood Cliffs, N.J.: Prentice-Hall,
1972.

Lorge, Irving. Psychology of Adults. Washington, D.C.:
Adult Education Association of the U.S.A., 1963.

Lumsden, D. Barry, and Ronald H. Sherron, eds. Experi-
mental Studies in Adult Learning and Memory.
Washington, D.C.: Hemisphere Publishing Co., 1975.

McClusky, Howard Y. "Adult Dimensions of Lifelong
Learning: Reflections on the Future of the Education Enterprise." Innovator 7, no. 9 (May 1976):
4-7.

McCoy, Vivian R. "Adult Life Cycle Change." Lifelong
    Learning: The Adult Years 1, no. 2 (October 1977):
    14-18, 31.

McCreary, Phyllis G., and John M. McCreary. Job Train-
    ing and Placement for Offenders and Ex-Offenders.
    Washington, D.C.: National Institute of Law En-
    forcement and Criminal Justice, U.S. Department of
    Justice, April 1975.

MacKenzie, Gordon N. "Curricular Change: Participants,
    Power, and Process." In Matthew B. Miles, ed.,
    Innovation in Education. New York: Teachers College
    Press, 1964. Pp. 399-424.

Mager, Robert F. Preparing Instructional Objectives.
    Palo Alto, Calif.: Fearon Publishers, 1962.

____. Preparing Objectives for Programmed Instruction.
    San Francisco: Fearon Publishers, 1961.

Mager, Robert F., and K. M. Beach. Developing Voca-
    tional Instruction. Belmont, Calif.: Fearon Pub-
    lishers, 1967.

Mass, H. S., and J. A. Kuypers. From Thirty to Seventy.
    San Francisco: Jossey-Bass, 1974.

Metfessel, Newton S., William B. Michael, and Donald
    A. Kirsner. "Instrumentation of Bloom's and Krath-
    wohl's Taxonomies for the Writing of Educational
    Objectives." Psychology in the Schools 6, no. 3
    (July 1969): 227-31.

Mezirow, J., G. G. Darkenwalk, and A. B. Know. Last
    Gamble on Education. Washington, D.C.: Adult Ed-
    ucation Association of the U.S.A., 1975.

Miller, Harry G., and Charles E. Greer. "Developing
    Adult Education Programs: Why? How?" Illinois
    School Board Journal 41, no. 1 (1973): 20-22.

Miller, Harry G., and John R. Verduin, Jr. The Adult
    Educator: A Handbook for Staff Development.
    Houston: Gulf Publishing Co., 1979.

Miller, Harry G. Teaching and Learning in Adult Educa-
    tion. New York: Macmillan Co., 1969.

Milne, Lorus J., and Margery Milne. The Ages of Life. New York: Harcourt Brace Jovanovich, 1968.

Nadler, Leonard. Developing Human Resources. Houston: Gulf Publishing Co., 1970.

O'Keefe, Michael. The Adult, Education and Public Policy. Palo Alto, Calif.: Aspen Institute for Humanistic Studies, 1976.

Parker, Stanley. The Future of Work and Leisure. New York: Praeger, 1971.

Paterson, R. W. K. Values, Education and the Adult. London: Routledge and Kegan Paul, 1979.

Peterson, Richard E., and Associates. Lifelong Learning in America. San Francisco: Jossey-Bass, 1979.

Phillips, J. Arch, Jr., and Richard Hawthorne. "Political Dimensions of Curriculum Decision Making." Educational Leadership 35, no. 5 (February 1978): 362-66.

Popham, W. James, and Eva L. Baker. Systematic Instruction. Englewood Cliffs, N.J.: Prentice-Hall, 1970.

Rauch, David B., ed. Priorities in Adult Education. New York: Macmillan Co., 1972.

Rogers, J. Adults Learning. Baltimore: Penguin Books, 1973.

Rosenberg, Geroge S. The Worker Grows Old. San Francisco: Jossey-Bass, 1970.

Salisbury, Robert H. "Schools and Politics in the Big City." Harvard Educational Review 37, no. 3 (Summer 1967): 408-24.

Scribner, Jay D., ed. The Politics of Education: 76th Yearbook of the National Society for the Study of Education. Chicago: University of Chicago Press, 1977.

Simpson, Elizabeth J. "The Classification of Educational Objectives in the Psychomotor Domain." In The Psychomotor Domain, Floyd Urbach, ed. Washington, D.C.: Gryphon House, 1972. Pp. 43-56.

Singer, Robert N., ed. The Psychomotor Domain: Movement Behaviors. Philadelphia: Lea and Febiger, 1972.

Smith, Edwin. Literacy Education for Adolescents and Adults. San Francisco: Boyd and Fraser, 1970.

Smith, Robert M., George F. Aker, and J. R. Kidd, eds. Handbook of Adult Education. New York: Macmillan Co., 1970.

Spears, Harold. "Kappans Ponder the Goals of Education." Phi Delta Kappan 55, no. 1 (September 1973): 29-32.

Taba, Hilda. Curriculum Development: Theory and Practice. New York: Harcourt, Brace and World, 1962.

Toffler, Alvin. Future Shock. New York: Random House, 1970.

Tough, Allen M. The Adult's Learning Projects: A Fresh Approach to Theory and Practice in Adult Learning. Toronto: Ontario Institute for Studies in Education, 1971.

Tuckman, Bruce W. Evaluating Instructional Programs. Boston: Allyn and Bacon, 1979.

Tyler, Ralph W. Principles of Curriculum and Instruction. Chicago: University of Chicago Press, 1950.

Ulmer, Curtis. Teaching the Disadvantaged Adult. Washington, D.C.: National Association for Public School Adult Education, 1969.

Venn, Grant. Man, Education and Manpower. Washington, D.C.: American Association of School Administrators, 1970.

Verduin, John R., Jr. Conceptual Models in Teacher Education: An Approach to Teaching and Learning. Washington, D.C.: American Association of Colleges for Teacher Education, 1967.

____. Cooperative Curriculum Improvement. Englewood
     Cliffs, N.J.: Prentice-Hall, 1967.

Verduin, John R., Jr., and Charles R. Heinz. Pre-
     Student Teaching Laboratory Experiences. Dubuque,
     Iowa: Kendall-Hunt Publishing Co., 1970.

Verduin, John R., Jr., Harry G. Miller, and Charles E.
     Greer. Adults Teaching Adults: Principles and
     Strategies. Austin, Tex.: Learning Concepts, 1977.

Vermilye, Dyckman W., ed. Relating Work and Education.
     San Francisco: Jossey-Bass, 1977.

Woodruff, Asahel D. "Putting Subject Matter into Con-
     ceptual Form." Paper prepared for TEAM Project
     meeting (which Project was sponsored by The Amer-
     ican Association of Colleges for Teacher Education),
     Washington, D.C., February 6, 1964.

Index

·